William Shaw

An Analysis of the Galic Language

Second Edition

William Shaw

An Analysis of the Galic Language
Second Edition

ISBN/EAN: 9783337084394

Printed in Europe, USA, Canada, Australia, Japan

Cover: Foto ©Paul-Georg Meister /pixelio.de

More available books at **www.hansebooks.com**

AN ANALYSIS

OF THE

GALIC LANGUAGE.

BY WILLIAM SHAW, A. M.

——— FORSAN ET HÆC OLIM MEMINISSE JUVABIT.
VIRG.

THE SECOND EDITION.

EDINBURGH.

Printed by W. and T. RUDDIMAN;
For R. JAMIESON, Parliament-square.

M,DCC,LXXVIII.

Entered in STATIONERS' HAL
According to Act of Parliament.

INTRODUCTION.

NATIONS by nature situated in the midst of the world, whatever their origin be, if they make any figure, and become considerable in peace or war, have their history, either by their own writers or those of other countries, transmitted to posterity; whilst the actions of people more remote, though perhaps not inferior in power, nor less considerable in peace, are lost in the oblivion of time, and their name and language almost annihilated or extinct. Of the latter sort is the Celtic nation. Situated early west of Greece and Rome, their learning and history, such powerful rivals having sprung up to the east of them, either remained with themselves, or emigrated from the continent to Britain and the adjacent islands.

Greece, at one time, subjecting the East, and Rome afterwards becoming mistress both of the East and West, the Galic power either decreased or retreated, and, in room of Galic, Roman learning succeeded. Rome, like every other great and wealthy state, by its own weight and unweildiness, dropt into non-existence; and now its language lives only

in

in books. An inundation of Barbarians from the northern parts overwhelmed the European continent. Letters, as affrighted, fled to the Hebrides and Ireland for an asylum, where they flourished for some centuries.

Saxon innovation, however, both in the northern and southern parts of Britain, proved fatal to the Galic power and language. The Cambrian and the Galic, formerly the same, but now different dialects of the Celtic, retreated, the one into Wales, and the other into the Highlands and western parts of Scotland. At the revival of letters, and afterwards at the Reformation in religion, the Galic, being unfortunately the provincial language of but a part of Scotland, and having ceased to be fashionable at court, did not partake of the advantages that other languages derive from the invention of printing. Under these disadvantages, however, it still is spoken with much purity, on a great part of the continent and islands of Scotland, and exists, at this day, one of the greatest living monuments of antiquity.

The human mind, with great longing, looks back into the past, less interested in many particulars of the present, which it overlooks, and of the future, which it enquires not after. The actions and connections, the fortune and habitations of our ancestors, the fields they walked on, their prudent conduct, and even foibles, we delight to hear recited, with an interested attention. The fields on which Cæsar, Alexander, and Fingal fought their battles;

the

INTRODUCTION. vii

the ruins of antient Rome, Carthage, Athens, or Palmyra; the contents of Herculaneum, a Grecian temple, an Egyptian pyramid, or Druidical circle; inspire the mind of every visitant with the ardent enthusiasm of inquiry, and a multitude of sorrowful thoughts on the instability of the highest temporal grandeur, which, attended by a pleasing melancholy, leaves the mind calmly pensive, and gently perplexed. But when I look back into the former times of the Gael, whose history a native might be supposed more immediately fond of, finding it so much involved in obscurity, or suppressed and obliterated by the policy of a neighbouring monarch, I could sit down and weep over its fall, execrating the policy of usurping invaders, ever destructive to letters, humanity, and its rights.

There are not, however, wanting, at this day, proofs sufficient to shew the Gael were once a very considerable people. As late as the Roman invasion, all that part of Britain north of the Tweed and Solway Frith, with several counties of South Britain, and all Ireland, with the adjacent islands, was inhabited by the Gael. When the Romans retired, and ceased to be a people, other invaders infested their coasts. The Danes, at different times, either invaded or conquered different parts of Britain, and as often were repulsed. The Saxons, however, having gained a settlement on the eastern coasts of South and North Britain, the Gael by degrees retreated to the north and western parts of Albin, as their invaders, the Scoti of the Low Countries, gained ground.

The

INTRODUCTION.

The different kingdoms of England, after some time, uniting and forming one great monarchy, became too powerful for the inhabitants of the Low Countries of Scotland, and obliged the Gael and the Gaill, or the strangers of the Low Countries, for the general security, likewise to become one, in opposition to the English. The seat of government, which fled before the Romans to the west and the islands, where the Palladium had hitherto remained secure, at this period having no enemy north of the Tweed, was removed to Scoone, afterwards to Dunfermling, thence to Edinburgh, and at last is arrived at Westminster. The Kings of Scotland, with the court, now residing in those parts where a dialect of the Saxon was spoken, and having in times of peace greater intercourse with the English, the Scots at length became the court language. From this period we may date the decline of the Galic.

All charters, deeds, records, and laws were now written in Latin or Scots. And the monasteries being pillaged by Edward, whatever was valuable in literature was entirely lost. Ireland, which hitherto was subjected by no foreign lord, nor distressed by the encroachments of a neighbouring state, except some temporary invasions by the Danes, quietly enjoyed the use of its laws, language, and liberties. It was at this juncture that the Irish Seanachies and annalists (when the Scots having thrown off their extorted allegiance to England, their annals and records being irrecoverably destroyed by Edward, wished to have some account of their own ori-

gin)

gin) invented their hyperbolic and incredible Milesian expedition from Egypt and Spain to Ireland, and thence to Scotland by the promontories of Galloway and Ceantire. Fordun, having no other materials, at once adopted this system, which gained universally in Scotland, until the ingenious Mr Macpherson published his Introduction to the History of Great Britain and Ireland. Whilst Roman learning, by the medium of a dialect of the Saxon, now flourished in Scotland, the Galic and Roman in some degree grew together in Ireland, which, for some centuries, was deemed the greatest school for learning in Europe. There letters and learned men, from all countries, found a secure retreat and asylum. Its happy situation, however, did not perpetuate these blessings. Ireland was invaded by the Danes, and, in a subsequent age, made subject to the Kings of England. Though there were English colonies in Ireland, the Gael of that country enjoyed their own laws and customs till the reigns of Elizabeth and James I. when the English laws were universally established. Then, for the first time, the Galic ceased to be spoken by the chiefs of families, and at court; and English schools were erected, with strict injunctions, that the vernacular language should no longer be spoken in these seminaries. This is the reason why the Iberno-Galic has more MSS. and books than the Caledonian. In Scotland there has been a general destruction of antient records and books, which Ireland escaped. It enjoyed its own laws and language till a later date, whilst the Scots-

English very early became the established language in North Britain.

In this situation I found the Galic, with few books, and fewer MSS. in the living voice of many thousands who entirely neglected it. The first Galic printed book ever known in Scotland, is the Irish translation of the Bible and New Testament. It underwent two impressions, one in the Irish, and the other in the Roman letter, but is now to be met with only in the libraries of the curious. Though the Bible be the common book of Christians, and to be met with in the language of every Protestant country, yet in Ireland and the Highlands of Scotland, it is at this day a curiosity. Notwithstanding that one-third of the ministers of the Church of Scotland, since the Reformation, daily preached in Galic, so little zeal for their own language prevailed, that the Bible is not yet translated; and it is within these ten years the New Testament has been attempted by one of their ministers. The Confession of Faith, and the Psalms in metre, both imitations of the Irish dialect, have been translated by the Synod of Argyle; and since, there have appeared three collections of songs and poems, all of which, though there be merit in the composition, are, however, wretchedly orthographied. By Mr Macdonald there has been a Vocabulary published at the expence of the Society for propogating Christian Knowledge in the Highlands, in which most things are expressed by circumlocution.

INTRODUCTION. xi

Mr Macfarlane, late minister at Killinvir, Argyleshire, translated Baxter's Call to the Unconverted. He understood the Galic well, and was a Grammarian; but his poetry is more forced than natural. Had others, however, been equally zealous, the language would have had many books, and been better understood by those who every day speak it. But at present I much doubt whether there be four men in Scotland that would spell one page the same way; for it has hitherto been left to the caprice and judgment of every speaker, without the steadiness of analogy or direction of rules. The taste, at this day, of the clergy, a lettered and respectable order, is to understand the English, content with what Galic enables them to translate a sermon they originally wrote in English. And although they are obliged to speak in public once in seven days, there are not five ministers in Scotland who write their discourses in their own tongue; yet there are several ambitious to be reputed the translators of a few lines of Galic poetry.

The improvement of the country, as well as the minds of the inhabitants, has been strangely neglected, in an age when every other country emerges from obscurity and ignorance, till some changes were forced upon them by a late law, I shall not say how politic. To see a people, naturally capable of every improvement, though once misled by ignorance, stripped of their ancient habits and customs, and deprived of the Scriptures in their own tongue, the right of Christians, never denied to the most savage

Indians,

Indians, is at once a complication of inhumanity and imprudence. Better flay their bodies to fecure their affections, as Rome was wont to do with heretics to bring their fouls to heaven, than keep them in ignorance, with the expectation that, after fome generations, the Englifh manners, language, and improvements, may begin to dawn. At this day, there is no equal number of people in Britain fo ufeful to the ftate. Upon every emergency they fupply our navy with good feamen, and our armies with valiant foldiers. But ftrip them of their drefs, language, the name and honour of Gael, and they foon degenerate. Their habit, language, life, and honour, they always kept or parted with at once. The honour of the name, their habit, and a Galic fpeech, have always infpired them more than the confecration of the colours. Government, by preferving thefe privileges, to them facred as their *aræ & foci*, might have at leaft one part of the community of whom they, on any emergency, might fay with the Roman general, " I know the tenth legion will not " defert me." From this I would infer, that the Gael fhould be taught to read the Scriptures in their own language, by which Popery, that ever grows in the foil of ignorance, might be for ever exterminated. Is there no Bifhop Bedel, no Robert Boyle in our days?

Conceiving an early tafte for Galic, on account of its peculiar beauties, when at the Univerfity, I thought, for my own private amufement, of fubjecting

ing it to certain rules, to be observed when I had occasion to speak it, an undertaking which, without any precedent, I thought at first impracticable.— Upon a more close attention, however to its peculiar genius, and the general philosophy of language, I found that

Nil tam difficile quod non solertia vincat;

and afterwards considering a Galic Grammar as an addition to the stores of literature, much wished for by many both in Scotland and England, I was encouraged to persevere in attempting to do what was never done before.

On the Iberno-Galic there have been written grammars by different hands. The Scots and Irish Galic, though not radically different, are two separate dialects of the same language. The words are almost always the same, but differently orthographied. The Irish, in their grammars, have a more uncertain and various inflection in the termination, which the Scots Galic has not; and this inclines me to think the Scots is the original, and that this inflection of termination in Irish grammars is the mark of an attempt by the monks to polish it, after the manner of the Greek and Latin.

Father O'Molloy published his *Grammatica Latina-Hibernica* in 12mo at Rome, 1677; and Macurtin, his Elements of the Irish, at Louvain, 1728: both of which merit only to be mentioned. There are many

INTRODUCTION.

many in MS. by various authors; but that published by the indefatigable Major Vallencia, in 1773, at Dublin, is the moſt ſatisfactory that has appeared.

In this treatiſe I have entirely confined myſelf to the Scots Galic, and think I have accounted for every phenomenon in its ſtructure. To reduce to rule a language without books, and having no ſtandard but the judgment of every ſpeaker, is an undertaking perhaps adventurous; but finding the alphabet conſiſting of eighteen letters, in which it has hitherto been written, ſo well adapted, that, with a very few combinations, every ſound in the language may be eaſily accommodated, it remained for me, after conſidering its genius, to raiſe this ſyſtem on that foundation. If, neverthelefs, it be found defective, it is altogether my own. I cannot, like other Grammarians, be called a compiler or tranſcriber; what I have delivered is the reſult of attentive obſervation. The books I found of moſt uſe are, Harris's *Hermes*, Sciopius's *Grammat. Philoſoph.* and particularly Mr Elphinſton's ingenious Analyſis of the Engliſh.

Being the firſt that has offered the public a grammatical account of the Galic, it was recommended by ſeveral perſons to frame a new alphabet, conſiſting of letters or combinations, to expreſs all the ſounds in the language, without any mute letter. This is impracticable; but though it could be effected, it would only render the etymology more perplexing. It was recommended to write *v* inſtead of *bh* and *mh*,

INTRODUCTION. xv

mo, and *y* instead of *dh* and *gh*; which if I had done, the inflections of words beginning with *b* and *m*, &c. would be indistinguishable. Thus, it could not be known whether *voladh* was praise, from *moladh*, praising; or *bholadh*, the dative of *boladh*, smell. Rejecting, for these and other reasons, all remarkable changes, I have only thrown away some useless consonants, retaining what are necessary to preserve the etymology and express the sounds. Excepting words that begin with certain consonants, the initial consonant before the aspirate *h*, there are no silent letters in the language. Unlike the Irish, the Scots Galic delights to pronounce every letter, and is not bristled over with so many useless and quiescent consonants. The English and French are infinitely more difficult to read and pronounce, and have many more silent and mute letters. In the Galic there are no such ugly looking words as *thought*, *through*, *strength*, &c. nor found so different from what the letters at other times express. How far I may have reduced it to a fixed system, founded on the general philosophy of language, and its own particular genius, others must determine; I only claim the indulgence always shewn to a juvenile attempt, especially of a passage through mountains never trod before. It was not the mercenary consideration of interest, nor perhaps the expectation of fame among my countrymen, in whose esteem its beauties are too much faded, but a taste for the beauties of the original speech of a now learned nation, that induced me either to begin, or encouraged me to persevere

in

in reducing to grammatical principles a language spoken only by imitation; while, perhaps, I might have been more profitably employed in tasting the various productions of men, ornaments of human nature, afforded in a language now teeming with books. I beheld with astonishment the learned in Scotland, since the revival of letters, neglect the Galic; as if it was not worthy of any pen to give a rational account of a speech used upwards of two thousand years by the inhabitants of more than one kingdom. I saw, with regret, a language once famous in the western world, ready to perish without any memorial, by the use of which Galgacus, having assembled his chiefs, rendered the Grampian Hills impassable to legions that had conquered the world; and by which Fingal inspired his warriors with the desire of immortal fame. I wished an account given to the world of a language, through which, for so long a period, the benefits of knowledge, and the blessings of religion were communicated to savage clans and roving barbarians, who, in past ages becoming civilized, sung the praises of Him who taught both the tongue to sound, and the thoughts to soar within the walls of the illustrious Iona.

Originally moved by these considerations, and at the request of many of the Literati, I have been encouraged to offer to the world what once I intended only for my own private use. A copy of the manuscript was desired by the Earl of EGLINTOUN, who has a taste for the language, as well as an attachment

to

to the people. I had the honour of presenting the original to his Lordship, without any expectation of its ever being published. Mr Boswell, whose manners as a gentleman, and taste for polite learning, have gained him the esteem and friendship, as well of one of the most renowned Heroes of the age, as of the learned at home, hearing from his Lordship of the existence of these sheets, obtained a perusal of them, which he afterwards left with Dr Samuel Johnson. To the advice and encouragement of Dr Johnson, the friend of letters and humanity, the Public is indebted for these sheets.

An acquaintance with the Galic, being the mother-tongue of all the languages in the west, seems necessary to every Antiquary who would study the affinity of languages, or trace the migrations of the ancient races of mankind. Of late it has attracted the attention of the learned in different parts of Europe; and shall its beauties be neglected by those who have opportunities, from their infancy, of understanding it? Antiquity being the taste of the age, some acquaintance with the Galic begins justly to be deemed a part of the *Belles Lettres*. The language that boasts of the finished character of Fingal, must richly reward the curiosity of whoever studies it. Of this Sir James Foulis is a rare instance, who, in advanced years, has learned to read and write it; and now drinks of the Pierian spring untainted, by reading fragments of Poetry in Fingal's own language.

INTRODUCTION.

If in thefe fheets I have afforded any gratification for curiofity, or any help to the Gael, in the improvement and ftudy of the language of their infant years, or prevented its dying without even a figh, I fhall think my labour well beftowed, and every attending trouble amply compenfated.

AN ANALYSIS OF THE GALIC LANGUAGE.

BOOK I.
CHAP. I.
ORTHOGRAPHY.

IN the Scots Galic are only eighteen letters, viz. *a, b, c, d, e, f, g, h, i, l, m, n, o, p, r, s, t, u,* divided into vowels and consonants. The Irish * wrote their dialect of the Celtic with these characters:

Aa, bb, Cc, Dd, Ee, Ff, Gg, Ii, Ll, Mm, Nn, Oo, Pp, Rr, Sr, Tt, Uu, hh.

The vowels are five, *a, e, i, o, u,* and are either broad or small: *a, o, u,* are broad, *e* and *i* are small.

---

* See Major Valencia's Grammar of the Irish.

CHAP. II.

Of the Sounds of the Vowels.

A is founded as with the Latins, broad; or as in the English words *fall, tall, call*; thus, *mall*, flow; *dall*, blind; *cam*, crooked; *aran*, bread.

Ao is founded as *u* in the French *une*; thus, *aon*, one, *une*; *aonach*, a fair or market, *unach*.

O is read as in the English *lord*, *opposite*; thus, *olc*, evil; *conn*, dun; *mor*, great; *morachd*, majesty: it is sometimes pronounced as in the French *foret*, Latin *forum*, and English *glory*; so *fonn*, a tune; *tonn*, a wave; *tom*, a bush.

U is founded as *oo* in the English *good, fool*; so *fudar*, powder; *udal*, distress; *ur*, new, &c.; some pronounce it as the consonant *u* in *uam*, saying *vuam*. It is changed into *V* in the proper name *Walter*, for we say *Valtair*.

E is pronounced as the Greek *epsilon*; thus, *edal*, a treasure. It is seldom alone in a syllable, but is generally followed by *a*, *u*, or *i*, and so forms a diphthong.

E, the pronoun *he*, is founded broad, like *eta* in the Greek, or as *e* in the English, *fellow, prunella*.

I has its natural sound, as the Latin *filius*, or the
French

French *fils*, and the English *feel*; so *innis*, an island; *imigh*, to go.

CHAP. III.

Of the Consonants.

B before *h* sounds *v*; thus, *leanabh*, a child, is read *leanav*; *leabhar*, a book, *leavar*; *labhairt*, speaking, *lavairt*.

C is equivalent to *k* in English, as *cos*, a foot; *cothrom*, just; *ceart*, right.

The pronunciation of the *c*, in some parts of the continent and islands, like *chg*, is certainly a corruption. Some dialects in Scotland still give it the natural sound of *k*, and so the Irish universally pronounce it. If there be no real difference between *chg* and *c*, why should they write *uchd* or *uchg*, the breast, and not *uc*; *lochd*, harm, and not *loc*; *naomhachd*, and not *naomhac*, since they write *mac*, but pronounce it *machd*, *breacan*, yet pronounce it *breachgan*, and *focal*, but pronounce it *fochgal?* The Irish rightly write *lochd*, *uchd*, *naomhachd*, &c. and pronounce them so; and *breacan*, *mac*, and *focal*, and pronounce *breakan*, *mak*, and *fokal*.

D before and after *e* and *i* is founded as *g* in the proper name *George*; thus, *dilis*, dear, is pronounced as if *jeelish*; *plaid*, a plaid or mantle, is pronounced *pladge*, or as the syllable *plaid* in the French *plaideur*;

Dia,

Dia, God, *Jeea*. After the broad vowels *a, o, u*, it is founded with the palate, as *da*, two; *do*, to him; *dubh*, black. *D* before *h* and after *i* in the termination of a word is mute, as *buanidh*, a reaper, *fgriobhidh*, will write; but *dh* in the beginning or middle of a word is pronounced as *y* in the English words *you, your, yellow, yawl*; thus, *dhuit*, to thee, is pronounced *yuit*; *dh'ol*, to drink, is nearly *yawl*. The termination *adh* is pronounced as *awy* in the word *lawyer*.

F before *h* is silent, as *an fhoid*, of the turf, we say *an hoid*; in other respects the same as in English.

G is founded as in the word *grow*.

1. Note, however, that *agh* in the beginning or termination of a word is read like *y* in *you, yawl*; as, *ghabh*, I took, is founded *yabh*, *gradhughadh*, loving, *grayachay*, (the *ay* being as *awy* in *lawyer*,) though the termination *adh* is founded *a* only.

2. *Agh, ugh*, are properly read in the middle of words *ach, uch*, or αχ, υχ, according to the Greek.

M before *h*, or *mh*, founds *v*, as *lamh*, a hand, *lav*; *claidhamh*, a sword, *clayav*; *mh* is mute in the pronoun *dhamh*, to me, and sometimes in the middle of words, though always written.

S before and after *e* and *i* is equivalent to *sh* in English;

English; thus *seol*, a sail, *sheol*; *innis*, an island, *innish*; *eisd*, hearken, *eishd*—Before and after *a*, *o*, *u*, the same as in English: thus, *tanas*, an apparition; *aslin*, a dream; *sugan*, a rope; *soillair*, clear; the pronoun *so*, this, pronounced *sho*, only excepted. S before *h* in the beginning of a word is always mute; as *shiubhal mi*, I went; *hiubhal mi* *.

P. *ph* is sounded *f* in the beginning of a word; *phobul*, to a people; *phosadh*, to marry; *phogadh*, to kiss.

T is sounded with the palate, but softer than in English. It is also mute before *h*; thus, *cruth*, a form or shape, *cruh*; *thuit*, he fell, *huit*; *thog*, he lifted, *hog*.

L, N, R, are immutable consonants, and never have the aspirate *h* after them in the past tenses of verbs, and the inflected cases of nouns, as the other letters, but seem then to be pronounced as if reduplicated; thus, *leabh*, I read, *lleabh*; *nairich*, he affronted, *nnairich*; *reub*, he tore, *rreub*.

Sg, sr, sp, st, do not obtain the *h* in the beginning of a word, but *tr* does, as *treoruidh*, direct thou; *threoruigh*, he directed.

Gn

---

* The late Rev. Mr. Macfarlane, who, of all the Highland Ministers, best understood the Orthography of the Galic, has, however, committed a very glaring mistake with regard to the letter S; he always writes *leiss*, *sibh*, *sin*, *sho*, instead of *leis*, *sibh*, *sin*, *so*.

Gn and *cn* in the beginning of words are often pronounced *gr* and *cr*; thus, *gnuis*, the countenance, is *gruis*; *cnaimh*, a bone, *craimh*; *bainionn*, female, *bairinn*.

CHAP. IV.

Of Diphthongs.

DIPHTHONGS are twelve, viz. *ao, ae, ai, ea, ei, eo, eu, ia, io, iu, oi, ua.*

Ai is founded as *ai* in the French *travailler*, to labour; thus, *pailtas*, plenty; *caill*, a loss; *faidh*, a prophet; *ait*, a place; *aitas*, gladness, &c.

Ea is founded like *ea* in the English *bear*, to bring; *bear*, the wild beast; as *feachran*, an error; *mear*, chearful, sportive; *fear*, a man; *bean*, a woman; *seanduine*, an old man; *feart*, authority. Sometimes like *ea* in the proper name *Lear*, and the verb *fear*; so *fearr*, better; *mearlach*, a thief; *feachd*, forces.

Ei sounds like *ai* in the word *sailor, fail*, or *a* in *pale, tale, male*, &c. so *eisd*, hearken; *teine*, fire; *fein*, self; *eiram*, I rise; *geimnach*, lowing.

Eo sounds as *eo* in the word *pigeon*; so *ceol*, music; *seol*, a sail; *beo*, alive.

In the diphthong *eu* the *u* serves only to lengthen the

the fignification or found of *e*; as *ceufadh*, a crucifixion, may be orthographied *ceifadh*; or as the *e* in *female*; *beus*, habit; *beul*, a mouth.

Ia has both letters heard in one fyllable; thus, *Dia* is one fyllable; *Diadhachd*, divinity, is but two; and *Diadomhnaich*, Sunday, three fyllables.

O! molaibh Dia, oir 'ta é maith!

Iu is founded like *oe* in *fhoe*, or *ew* in *ftew*; thus, *iul*, a guide, is read *ewl*; *fiubhalam*, I go or pafs, *fhewvalam*; *ciuil*, of mufic, *cewl*; *fiu*, worthy, *few*; *fiucar*, fugar, *fhewcar*.

Io is pronounced like an *i* long, or *ee* in Englifh; as in *feel, fees, lees*; or *i* in the French *Sire, filence*, &c. as *anios*, up; *fios*, knowledge; *fior*, true; *fioridh*, for ever; *ionnas*, treafure.

Oi is founded like *oi* in *oil, foil, foil*,—*oigh*, a virgin; *coill*, a wood; *moidhach*, an hare; *foighdair*, a foldier.

Ua has both vowels pronounced in one fyllable; fo *fuar*, cold; *fuas*, up; *anuas*, down; *ruadh*, red; *ag tuar*, foreboding, &c.

In *ui*, the *u* is long and *i* heard, or founded like *oo* in *fool, good, food*; fo *fuil*, blood; *fuil*, the eye; *cuil*, of the back; *muill*, of chaff, &c.

D CHAP.

CHAP. V.

Of Triphthongs.

THERE are these five triphthongs, *aoi, eoi, eai, iui, uai;* the two first vowels of which are of the diphthongs already mentioned, sound the same, and the third vowel is heard; as in these words, *aois,* age; *maoisach,* a fallow-deer or doe; *feoil,* flesh; *stiuir,* a rudder or helm; *iuil,* of a guide; *uait,* from thee; *duais,* a reward; *cluais,* of an ear.

The above observations with regard to orthography will, I apprehend, with the assistance of a few books, not only be sufficient to preserve this copious and expressive language, but make a stranger better acquainted with it in one month, than he could be with the English or French in six, by consulting all that has been written on either of these subjects.

We will now give a small collection of words divided into syllables, for the use and practice of the Reader, writing the same in an opposite column, spelled according to assistance taken from, and reference made to, the French and English, to express their sounds. Let this mark * distinguish French-like syllables, and this ┼ the English.

An-

THE GALIC LANGUAGE.

An-eo-lach,	áin-eo-lach,	ignorant.
Ainm-ol,	ainm-ol,	renowned.
Cint-ach,	cint-ach,	sure.
Diomh-an-ach,	jeev-an-ach,	idle.
Deas-shoc-lach,	jeas-oc-lach,	witty.
Mio-chaird-ol,	mee-char-jol,	unfriendly.
Eud-mhor,	aid-vor,	jealous.
Aidh-ear-ach,	ay-ar-ach,	glad.
Aol-tigh,	aol-toy,	a college.
Sgiob-al-te,	sgee-bal-ta,	neat, tight.
Di-cia-daoine,	jee-cia-daogne,	Wednesday.
Ball-leath-air,	ball-lea-ir,	a goff-ball.
Sgoth-long,	scoh-long,	a yacht.
Cain-adh,	caign-ay,	scandalizing.
Feoirn an,	feoir-nan,	a straw.
Sdiuir-adh,	stew-ray,	steering at the helm.
Fuaidh-al,	foy-al,	sewing.

These words comprehend most of the sounds in the language, and are pretty nearly expressed as marked in the second column.

AN

AN ANALYSIS OF THE GALIC LANGUAGE.

BOOK I.
CHAP. I.
OF ETYMOLOGY.

Of Nouns Substantive.

THE parts of speech are eight—Noun, Pronoun, Verb, Participle, Adverb, Preposition, Interjection, Conjunction.

The Genders are two, Masculine and Feminine; that is, *e* or *i*, *he* or *she*.

Since the Galic language personifies every object, inanimate as well as animate, the distinction of gender is the principal difficulty; and this is what renders the Gael's first attempts to speak English so ridiculous,

diculous, every substantive being either *e* or *i*, that is, *he* or *she*. Neither termination (except that all nouns in *og* and *ag* are feminine), nor any other circumstance but immediate distinction of sex, and custom, can determine the gender. They talk of a *stone*, a *spoon*, a *window*, a *fiddle*, a *shoe*, a *hat*, a *chair*, and a *knife*, as a *she*; but a *stocking*, a *coat*, a *stool*, a *fork*, as *he* or *it*. Nouns, however, having *a* alone in the last syllable, before one or more final consonants, are generally masculine; as, *aodan*, a face; *abhar*, a cause; *cogadh*, war, &c.

Nouns having *o* in the last syllable are generally masculine; as, *corp*, a body; *ceo*, mist; *bord*, a board; *bonn*, the sole, or base of any thing.

Nouns which have a diphthong in termination, the last vowel of which is broad, are generally masculine; as, *beul*, a mouth; *meall*, an heap; *gaoth*, the wind, &c.

Nouns which have a diphthong in termination, the last vowel of which is slender, are feminine; as, *uine*, time; *uair*, an hour; *cuis*, an affair; *compailt*, a company, &c.

Agents in *air* and *oir* are masculine: all nouns in *og* and *ag* are feminine.

The Numbers are two, Singular and Plural; as, *moidhach*, a hare; *moidhaich*, hares; *fiadh*, a deer; *feidh*, deer.

There

THE GALIC LANGUAGE.

There are six Cases, Nominative, Genitive, Dative, Accusative, Vocative, and Ablative—in Galic, *Ainminach, Geinmheanach, Tabhartach, Gioranach, Gairminach,* and *Diobhalach.*

The Declensions are two.

1. Nouns of the first declension have the nominative plural like their genitive singular; as, *moidhach,* a hare; genitive, *moidhaich,* of a hare; nominative plural, *moidhaich,* hares.

2. Nouns of the second declension have their nominative plural in *a* or *an;* as, *cretoir,* an animal; plural, *cretoira,* or *cretoiran,* animals. At the same time, every noun is either definite or indefinite, that is, declined with or without the article. Indefinitely thus, *moidhach,* a hare; definitely, *am moidhach,* the hare; *cretoir,* an animal; *an cretoir,* the animal.

The Article.

	Singular.		Plural.	
	Masc.	Fem.	Masc.	Fem.
N.	an,	an, (or) a'.	na,	na.
G.	an,	na.	nan,	nan.
D.	do'n,	do'n.	do na,	do na.
A.	an,	an (or) a'.	na,	na.
V.	o! an,	o! an.	o! na,	o! na.
A.	leis an,	leis an (or) a'.	leis na,	leis na.
	Aans an,	anns an (or) anns a'.	anns na,	anns na.

The

The article *an* masculine of the nominative and accusative singular, is changed to *am* before nouns beginning with *f, b,* and *p,* if the noun be masculine. If the noun begins with a vowel, the letter *t* is prefixed in the nominative and accusative; as, *an t ord,* the hammer; if with an *s,* as *flat,* a rod or wand, *an t flat,* the *s* being silent. *Nan* of the genitive plural before *f, b, p,* is changed to *nam;* before a noun beginning with a *c* or *g,* is sounded as if the last *n* were joined to the *g;* as *nan ceum,* of the steps, *na nceum; nan cos,* as if *na ncos.* When the noun is masculine, and begins with an *f,* the euphonic *t* is retained in the genitive, dative, and ablative singular; as, *faol,* the world, genitive, *an t faoil;* dative, *d'on t faol;* ablative, *leis an t faol:* but if feminine, it is retained throughout the whole singular, except the genitive case; as, nominative, *an t flat,* the wand; dative, *do'n t flat;* accusative, *an t flat;* vocative, *o' an t flat;* ablative, *leis an t flat.* But this is only when it is definitely declined.

General Rules.

The Nominative and Accusative are always alike in both numbers.

Do is the sign of the dative; *le* or *leis* of the ablative.

All definite names have the article; indefinites have not.

The flection of a Celtic noun does not, like a Greek noun, consist in an inflected article and termination only; nor a Roman noun, with its termination inflected; nor like the French, English, or Italian, in particles; nor yet like a * Hebrew noun, in syntax; but is declined definitely, with an article, a change of the vowel or diphthong of its termination, and by introducing the aspirate *h* after the initial consonant. Thus, *am moidhach*, the hare; genitive, *an mhoidhaich*, of the hare; dative, *do'n mhoidbach*, to the hare, &c. or indefinitely, dative, *do' mhoidhach*, to a hare; genitive, *moidhaich*, of a hare.

A Forma, or Scheme, shewing the Changes of the mutable Consonants in the Inflection both of Nouns and Verbs.

a
b———*bh*, which sounds like *v* in English.
c———*ch*, always a guttural sound.
d———*dh*, resembles *y* in English.
e
f———*fh*, in which *f* is silent; *do*, the sign of the dative in nouns and past tenses of verbs beginning with *f*, is

best

---

* At casus non actu, sed potestate, hic sunt, id est, non diversarum terminationum, sed ex structura sermonis; neque etiam articulis aut notis discernuntur, sed omnino ex syntaxi di judicandi sunt. Buxt. Gram. Heb.

beſt wrote thus, *fianuis*, a witneſs; dative, *dſhianuis*, to a witneſs; *fiosrucham*, I inquire; *dſhioſruich mi*, I inquired; *f* is ſilent, *dh* ſounded like *y*; thus, *yeſruich mi*.

g———*gh*, like *dh*, reſembles *y*.
h
i

l———*l* ſeems to ſound like *ll*; ſo *labhram*, I ſpeak; *labhair mi*, I ſpake; *llabhair mi*.

m———*mh*, ſounds like *v*, but more labial than *bh*. The reader who underſtands Galic may prove this by comparing the words *lamh* and *labhair*.

n——— like *l* ſeems as if reduplicated.
o

p———*ph* ſounds like *f*.
r——— like *n* and *l*, ſeems reduplicated.
ſ———*ſh*, of which *ſ* is mute, and *h* has its full force.
t———*th*, of which *t* is ſilent and *h* ſounded.

Example of a Noun of the firſt Declenſion, Indefinite, and of the Maſculine Gender.

Singular.

N. *Moidhach*, a hare.
G. *Moidhaich*, of a hare.
D. *Do mhoidhach*, to a hare.
A. *Moidhach*, a hare.
V. *Mhoidhaich!* O hare!
A. *Le moidhach*, with a hare.

Plural.

Plural.

N. *Moidhaich*, hares.
G. *Mhoidhach*, of hares.
D. *Do mhoidhaich*, to hares.
A. *Moidhaich*, hares.
V. *Mhoidhaich!* O hares!
A. *Le mhoidhaich*, with hares.

Definitely, or with the Article.

Singular.

N. *Am moidhach*, the hare.
G. *A' mhoidhaich*, of the hare.
D. *Do'n mhoidhach*, to the hare.
A. *Am moidhach*, the hare.
V. *O am moidhach!* O the hare!
A. *Leis a' mhoidhach*, with the hare.

Plural.

N. *Na moidhaich*, the hares.
G. *Nam moidhach*, of the hares.
D. *Do na moidhaich*, to the hares.
A. *Na moidhaich*, the hares.
V. *O na moidhaich!* O the hares!
A. *Leis na moidhaich*, with the hares.

The most common terminations of this declension are, *adh*, *ach*, and all patronymicks and gentiles which end in *ach*; as, *Albanach*, a Scotsman; *Eirinach*, an Irishman; *Muilach*, an Isle of Mull Man; *Boidach*, a Bute Man; *Arrunach*, an Arran man; *Lochlunach*,

Lochlunach, a Dane; *Francach*, a Frenchman; *Spainach*, a Spaniard; *Feudailtach*, an Italian; *Caimbeulach*, a Campbell; *Stuartach*, a Stuart; *Friofalach*, a Fraser: *Grantach*, a Grant; *Gordanach*, a Gordon; *Donalach*, a Macdonald, &c. In the plural, *Albanaich, Eirinaich, Muilaich, Boidaich, Arrunaich, Lochlunaich, Francaich, Spainaich, Feudailtaich, Caimbeulaich, Stuartaich, Friofalaich, Grantaich, Gordanaich, Donalaich,* &c. Scotsmen, Irishmen, Mullmen, Butemen, Arranmen, Danes, French, Spaniards, Italians, Campbells, Stuarts, Frasers, Grants, Gordons, Macdonalds, &c. Some end in *an*; as, *fuaran*, a spring; *fuarain*, springs;—some in *ull*; as *capull*, a mare, *capuil*:—some in *adh*, such as, *cruinuchadh*, a congregation, *cruinuchaidh*; *fioladh*, a syllable, *fiolaidh*; *fluagh*, an host, *floigh*:—and some in *as*; as, *iongantas*, a wonder, *iongantais*; *neual*, a cloud, has *neoil*; *eun*, a bird, *eoin*; *cnoc*, a hill, *cnoic*; *mac*, a son, *mic*; *tarbh*, a bull, *tairbh*; *cliabh*, a basket, *cleabh*. Nouns which have their nominative plural the same as their genitive singular, are also of this declension. There are many nouns used by provincialists in the plural of both declensions; such as, *mairt*, or *marta*, cattle, kine; *cuirp* or *corpa*, bodies, &c.

The Rev. Mr Macfarlane, in his translations and psalms, uniformly uses *ibh* in the dative and ablative plural; which I think too much resembles the Irish dialect. *Do na Muilaichibh, leis na Caimbeulaichibh,* would have a harsh sound to any provincialist of Scotland.

Of

THE GALIC LANGUAGE. 37

Of the Singular Indefinite of both Declensions.

The Genitive singular indefinite is formed by putting an *i* after the last vowel of the nominative; as, *fuaran*, a spring; genitive, *fuarain*. But if the nown has *i* in the nominative, the same is the genitive; as, *cuisle*, a vein; genitive, *cuisle*, of a vein: *crios*, a girdle; genitive, *crios*.

Nouns in *iabh* and *iath* change *ia* into *ea* in the genitive, as *sliabh*, a mountain; genitive *sleabh*, of a mountain: *cliabh*, a basket, the chest or breast; genitive, *cleabh*: *sgiath*, a wing: genitive, *sgeath*, of a wing: *Dia*, God; genitive, *Dea*.

Nouns in *iar* and *ial* form *ei* in the genitive; as, *cial*, wisdom, *ceil*; *ciar*, *ceir*. Those in *ean*, *eal*, *eac*, change the diphthong *ea* into *i* in the genitive; as *ceann*, a head; genitive, *cinn*, of a head: *meall*, an heap; genitive, *mill*: *leac*, a slate; genitive, *lic*.

Monosyllables beginning with an *a* or *o*, change them into *ui* in the genitive; as *alt*, a joint; genitive *uilt*, of a joint: *ord*, a hammer; genitive *uird*: *bonn*, a base or coin; genitive, *buinn*.

Nouns in *ta*, *de*, *ca*, *pa*, have the genitive like the nominative; as, *cota*, a coat; *cloica*, a clock; *colpa*, the leg; *plaide*, a plaid.

Monosyllables having *a*, *o*, or *u* after an initial consonant, change these into *ui* in the genitive; as *ball*, a ball, or any member of the body, a place; genitive, *buill*: *moll*, chaff; genitive, *muill*: *cul*, the back; genitive, *cuil*.

The

The Dative singular is formed from the Nominative, by putting the letter *h* after the initial consonant, and prefixing the sign *do*; as, *moidhach*, a hare; dative, *do mhoidhach*: *cretoir*, an animal; dative, *do chretoir*.

When the Nominative begins with a vowel, *dh* prefixed is the sign of the dative; as *ord*, a hammer; dative, *dh'ord*: *oran*, a song; dative, *dh'oran*.

The Vocative is formed from the genitive, by putting *h* after the initial consonant; as, genitive, *moidhaich*: vocative, *mhoidhaich*; *cretoir*, of an animal; vocative, *chretoir*, O animal!

If the noun begins with a vowel, the vocative is like the genitive; as genitive, *uird*; vocative *uird*: *Eoin*, of John, John's; vocative, *Eoin*, O John!

Of the Plural of the first Declension, indefinitely.

Nouns in *adh*, *ach*, *an*, *ull*, which are the most common terminations of this declension, and some monosyllables, have their nominative plural like the genitive singular; as *cruinuchadh*; genitive, *cruinuchaidh*; nominative plural, *cruinuchaidh*: genitive, *moidhaich*; nominative plural, *moidhaich*: genitive, *fuarain*; nominative plural, *fuarain*; *capuill*, of a mare; nominative plural, *capuill*, mares.

The Genitive has *h* after the initial consonant; as *mhoidhach*, *chruinuchadh*, *fhuaran*, *chapull*.

*Do bhrat lan fhraddag daimond
Do bhraon ni foils' air lar* *.

If the Nominative singular begins with a vowel or diphthong, the genitive plural is the same; as *fuaim ord*, the noise of hammers.

The Vocative plural of this declension is the same as the vocative singular; *mhoidhaich*, O hare! *mhoidhaich*, hares!

The Dative is formed by adding the *h* flection to to the nominative plural; *moidhaich; do mhoidhaich*.

Of Definites of the first Declension.

The Genitive singular definite of nouns in *adh*, *ach*, &c. of this declension, is formed from the vocative singular indefinite, by putting the article *an* or *a'* before it; as vocative indefinite, *mhoidhaich;* genitive definite, *a' mhoidhaich*, of the hare; *eoin*, O bird! *an eoin*, of the bird.

But if the noun be of the feminine, *h* is thrown away, and its feminine article put before it; as vocative indefinite, *ghealaich*, O moon! genitive definite, *na gealaich*, of the moon.

Nouns

---

* Macdonald's *Alt an t fhucair*, a most beautiful Description of a rural Scene.

Nouns beginning with the immutable consonants *l, n, r*, never admit the flection *h;* as *leabhair*, of a book; definite, *an leabhair*, of the book, &c.

The Dative definite is like the dative indefinite, having the article before it; as, *do mhoidhach;* definite, *do'n mhoidhach*, to the hare. If the noun begins with a *d* or *t*, the *h* is omitted; as, *do'n damh, do'n tarbh*.

The Vocative is like the nominative; as, *am moidhach, O am moidhach!*

Of the second Declension Indefinite.

Masculine Gender. Singular Number.

N. *Cretoir*, an animal.
G. *Cretoir*, of an animal.
D. *Do chretoir*, to an animal.
A. *Cretoir*, an animal.
V. *O! chretoir*, O animal!
A. *Le cretoir*, with an animal.

Plural.

N. *Cretoira*, or *cretoiran*, animals.
G. *Chretoira*, of animals.
D. *Do chretoira*, to animals.
A. *Cretoira*, animals.
V. *O chretoira!* O animals!
A. *Le cretoira*, with animals.

Definitely.

THE GALIC LANGUAGE.

Definitely.

Singular.

N. *An cretoir*, the animal.
G. *A' chretoir*, of the animal.
D. *Do'n chretoir*, to the animal.
A. *An cretoir*, the animal.
V. *O an cretoir!* O the animal!
A. *Leis an chretoir*, with the animal.

Plural.

N. *Na cretoira*, the animals.
G. *Nan cretoira*, of the animals.
D. *Do na cretoira*, to the animals.
A. *Na cretoira*, the animals.
V. *O na cretoira!* O the animals!
A. *Leis na cretoira*, with the animals.

Indefinitely.

Singular.

N. *Offag*, a blast.
G. *Offaig*, of a blast.
D. *Dh' offag*, to a blast.
A. *Offag*, a blast.
V. *Offaig*, O blast!
A. *Le offag*, with a blast.

Plural.

N. *Offaga*, blasts.
G. *Offaga*, of blasts.
D. *Dh' offaga*, to blasts.
A. *Offaga*, blasts.

V. *Offaiga*,

V. *Offaiga*, O blasts!
A. *Le offaga*, with blasts.

Definitely.

Singular.
N. *An offag*, the blast.
G. *Na h offaig*, of the blast.
D. *Do'n offag*, to the blast.
A. *An offag*, the blast.
V. *O! an offag*, O the blast!
A. *Leis an offag*, with the blast.

Plural.
N. *Na h offaga*, the blasts.
G. *Nan offaga*, of the blasts.
D. *Do na h offaga*, to the blasts.
A. *Na h offaga*, the blasts.
V. *O! n h offaga*, O the blasts!
A. *Leis na h offaga*, with the blasts.

All other nouns, except those noted of the first, are of this declension, the most common terminations of which are these, *ad, aid, air, ar, eir, ir, or;* some in *an;* also *ill, il, os, ath, unt, iu, og, ag, in, ain, airt, ub, uth, is, eis, idh.*

Of Definites of the Second Declension.

So much having been said under the first declension, and the difference of the second being so small, little remains to be observed here; I shall therefore only note a few particulars of the second.

If the Noun be of the feminine gender, the genitive definite is formed from the indefinite, by prefixing the article *na*; as, *cois*, of a foot; genitive definite, *na cois*, of the foot. And if the noun feminine begins with a vowel, the letter *h* is prefixed, to shun the hiatus; thus, *ailne*, beauty; genitive definite, *na h ailne*, of the beauty: *eagnai*, wisdom; genitive definite, *na h eagnai*, of the wisdom.

Nouns beginning with the immutable consonants *l, n, r,* do not admit of the flection *h*; so *rinnag*, a star; genitive, *rinnaig*, of a star; definite, *na rinnaig*, of the star.

Of the Plural definite of both Declensions.

All nouns of this declension have their nominative plural in *a* or *an*; and when the word following begins with a vowel, rather in *an*; so *laoidh*, an hymn, *laoidha*, hymns; *treud*, a flock, *treuda*; *ionad*, a place, *ionada*; *palluin*, a temple or palace, *palluina*; *dorus*, a door, *doruisa*, contracted *dorsa*; *namhaid*, an enemy, *namhaida*, contracted *naimhda*; *coinnal*, a candle, *coiunlan*, by elision of the *a*; *crioch*, an end, or the limits of any thing, *criocha*; *oigh*, a virgin, *oigha*; *machair*, a field, *machaira*; *mue*, a sow, *muca*; *anam*, a soul, *anama*; *claidhamh*, a sword, *claidhamha*; *targaid*, a target, *targaida*; *lamh*, an hand, *lamha*; *beannachd*, a blessing, or compliments, *beannachda*; *triobloid*, trouble, *triobloda*; *cloch*, a stone, *clocha*; *craobh*, a tree, *craopha*; *carruig*, a rock, *carruiga*;

piobair,

piobair, a piper, *piobaira*; *fiadhnuis*, a witness, *fiadhnuisa*; *ossag*, a blast, *ossaga*; *sguab*, a sheaf, *sguaba*; *uinog*, a window, *uinoga*; *gaoth*, the wind, *gaotha*.

The genitive definite plural of nouns of the first declension is formed by prefixing *nam*, or *nan*, the article, to the nominative singular indefinite: of the second, by prefixing it to its nominative plural, and sometimes the termination is dropt; as, *moidhach, nam moidhach, cretoira, nan cretoira*.

Some Nouns ending in *a* in the singular, change *a* into *icha* or *in* in the plural; as *cota*, a coat, *coticha, cotin*; *plaid*, a plaid, *plaidicha, plaidin*; *uisge*, has sometimes *uisge*, oftener *uisgicha*; *eige*, a web, *eigicha*; *leine*, a shirt, *leintach, leintin*; *sliabh*, a mountain, *sleabhte*. The terminations *idh*, and *ich*, have *icha*; as, *buanidh*, a reaper, *buanicha*; *ramhich*, a rower, *ramhicha*.

Proper Names are thus declined:

N. *Ceantir*, Kintyre.
G. *Chintir*, of Kintyre.
D. *Do Cheantir*, to Kintyre.
A. *Ceantir*, Kintyre.
V. *Chintir*, O Kintyre!
A. *Le Ceantir*, with Kintyre.

N. *Ossian*,

N. *Offian*, Offian.
G. *Offain*, of Offian.
D. *Dh' Offian*, to Offian.
A. *Offian*, Offian.
V. *Offiain!* O Offian!
A. *Le Offian*, with Offian.

N. *Treunmor*, Trenmore.
G. *Threinmhoir*, of Trenmore.
D. *Do Threunmor*, to Trenmore.
A. *Treunmor*, Trenmore.
V. *Threinmhoir!* O Trenmore!
A. *Le Treunmor*, with Trenmore.

Proper names of places are Feminine.

Irregulars.

Indefinite.

Singular.	Plural.
N. *Bean*, a woman.	*Mnàn*, women.
G. *Mna*, of a woman.	*Mhnàn*, of women.
D. *Do bhean, do mhnaoi*, to a woman.	*Do mhnan*, to women.
A. *Bean*, a woman.	*Mnan*, women.
V. *Bhean!* O woman!	*O! mhnan!* O women!
A. *Le bean, le mnaoi*, with a woman.	*Le mnan*, with women.

Fuil, blood, has *fola* in the genitive; *feoil*, flesh, has *feola*; *dutchich*, a country, *ducha*; and *leaba*, a bed, has *leape*, by way of interchange. *Dutchich* in the plural has *duchana*; *leabe* has *leapucha*; *baile*, a town,
has

has *bailte*; *mile*, a mile, or a thousand, has *milte*; and *ni*, a thing, has *nithe*; and *fine*, a nation, family, clan, or tribe, has *finacha*; *gniomh*, a deed, *gniomha*, and *gniomhara*.

CHAP. II.

Of Adjectives.

AS the flection that a Noun Substantive undergoes in the singular, is the introduction of an *i* into the termination (if there be more than one syllable), and putting the aspirate *h* after the initial consonant; the same flection must the adjective undergo to agree with its substantive. On the concord of adjectives and substantives, the following observations are to be considered:

1st. When the termination of a noun ends in *a* or *an* in the plural, the adjective agreeing with that case, has no *h* aspirate nor flection in its own termination; as, *na claidhamha mor*, the broad swords; *na paisdan beg*, the little children. The same holds good, when any case of nouns of the first declension is changed to *an* or *a*; as for, *na fuarain, na fuarana*, &c.

2d. The *h* aspirate of the substantive noun is retained by the adjective, and throughout the cases; as, as, *moidhaich moir*, of a great hare; definite, *a' mhoidhaich mhoir*, of the great hare.

3d. Nouns of the first declension have the *h* flection in the plural; but never any in termination.

Example of an Adjective and Substantive of the first Declension. Indefinite.

Singular.

N. *Moidhach mor*, a large hare.
G. *Moidhaich mor*, of a large hare.
D. *Do mhoidhach mhor*, to a large hare.
A. *Moidhach mor*, a large hare.
V. *Mhoidhaich mhoir*, O large hare!
A. *Le moidhach mor*, with a large hare.

Plural.

N. *Moidhaich mhor*, large hares.
G. *Mhoidhach mhor*, of large hares.
D. *Do mhoidhaich mhor*, to large hares.
A. *Moidhaich mhor*, large hares.
V. *Mhoidhaich mhor*, O large hares!
A. *Le moidhaich mhor*, with large hares.

Definite.

Singular.

N. *Am moidhach mor*, the large hare.
G. *A' mhoidhaich mhoir*, of the large hare.

D. *Do'n*

D. *Do'n mhoidhach mhor*, to the large hare.
A. *Am moidhach mor*, the large hare.
V. *O am moidhach mor!* O the large hare!
A. *Leis a' mhoidhach mhor*, with the large hare.

Plural.

N. *Na moidhaich mhor*, the large hares.
G. *Nam moidhach mor*, of the large hares.
D. *Do na moidhaich mhor*, to the large hares.
A. *Na moidhaich mhor*, the large hares.
V. *O na moidhaich mhor!* O the large hares!
A. *Leis na moidhaich mhor*, with the large hares.

Examples of the second Declension.

Singular.

N. *Cretoir maifach*, an handsome animal.
G. *Cretoir maifaich*, of an handsome animal.
D. *Do chretoir mhaifach*, to an handsome animal.
A. *An cretoir maifach*, an handsome animal.
V. *Chretoir mhaifaich!* O handsome animal!
A. *Le cretoir maifach*, with an handsome animal.

Plural.

N. *Cretoira maifach*, handsome animals.
G. *Chretoira maifach*, of handsome animals.
D. *Do chretoira maifach*, to handsome animals.
A. *Cretoira maifach*, handsome animals.
V. *Chretoira maifach!* O handsome animals!
A. *Le cretoira maifach*, with handsome animals.

Definitely.

THE GALIC LANGUAGE.

Definitely.

Singular.

N. *An cretoir maifach*, the handsome animal.
G. *A' chretoir mhaifaich*, of the handsome animal.
D. *Do'n chretoir mhaifach*, to the handsome animal.
A. *An cretoir maifach*, the handsome animal.
V. *O an cretoir maifach!* O the handsome animal!
A. *Leis a' chretoir mhaifach*, with the handsome animal.

Plural.

N. *Na cretoira maifach*, the handsome animals.
G. *Nan cretoira maifach*, of the handsome animals.
D. *Do na cretoira maifach*, to the handsome animals.
A. *Na cretoira maifach*, the handsome animals.
V. *O na cretoira maifach!* O the handsome animals!
A. *Leis na cretoira maifach*, with the handsome animals.

A Noun Feminine and an Adjective.

Singular.

N. *Offag mhor*, a great blast.
G. *Offaig moir*, of a great blast.
D. *Dh' offag mhor*, to the great blast.
A. *Offag mhor*, a great blast.
V. *Offaig mhoir!* O great blast!
A. *Le offag mhor*, with a great blast.

G Plural.

Plural.

N. *Offaga mor*, great blasts.
G. *Offaga mor*, of great blasts.
D. *Dh' offaga mor*, to great blasts.
A. *Offaga mor*, great blasts.
V. *Offaga mor !* O great blasts !
A. *Le offaga mor*, with great blasts.

Definite.

Singular.

N. *An offag mhor*, the great blast.
G. *Na h offaig moir*, of the great blast.
D. *Do'n offag mhor*, to the great blast.
A. *An offag mhor*, the great blast.
V. *O an offag mhor!* O the great blast !
A. *Leis an offag mhor*, with the great blast.

Plural.

N. *Na h offaga mor*, the great blasts.
G. *Nan offaga mor*, of the great blasts.
D. *Do na h offaga mor*, to the great blasts.
A. *Na h offaga mor*, the great blasts.
V. *O na h offaga mor!* O the great blasts !
A. *Leis na h offaga mor*, with the great blasts.

Of Comparison.

THERE are three degrees of Comparison; the Positive, Comparative, and Superlative.

The Comparative is formed from the genitive singular indefinite of the positive; *i. e.* by making the last vowel an *i*, and adding *e* to the positive; thus, *laidir*, strong; genitive indefinite, *laidir*; comparative, *laidire*, stronger; *luachmhor*, precious; genitive indefinite, *luachmhoir*; comparative, *luachmhoire*, more precious: *dubh*, black; *duibhe*, blacker: *geal*, white; comparative, *gile*, whiter. It is resolved by *no*, than, the conjunction.

The Superlative is like the Comparative, and is distinguished only by the words that follow, and are governed by it; as, *laidire agibh*, the strongest of you; *luach-mhoire dhin*, the most precious of us; *duibhe acca*, blackest of them; *gile aginne*, the whitest of us; *maisiche am measg an t sluaigh*, handsomest among the people. The particle *ro* put before any adjective is equal to the English *very* or *most*, the French *tres*, and the Latin *per*; thus, *ro bheartach*, very or most rich; *tres* or *fort riche*; *perdives:* *ro bhochd*, very or most poor; *bien, tres,* or *fort pauvre*; *perpauper*. Note, that neither the comparative nor the superlative undergo any change by flection.

Irregulars.

Irregulars.

Positive.	Comparative.	Superlative.
Maith,	fearr,	fearr (or) ro mhaith.
Good,	better,	best.
Olc,	mease,	mease, ro olc.
Evil,	worse,	worst.
Mor,	moa,	moa (or) ro mhor.
Great,	greater,	greatest, most great.
Beg,	lughe,	lughe, ro bheg.
Little,	less,	least, very little.
Gairrid,	giurra,	giurra, ro ghairrid.
Short,	shorter,	shortest.
Leathan,	leatha,	leatha, ro leathan.
Broad,	broader,	broadest.

CHAP. III.

Of Pronouns.

AS the Prepositions that generally govern different cases are so united with the simple pronouns (though still their composition may be seen), I think it most proper to write them as one word, without any mark of contraction.

Singular.

THE GALIC LANGUAGE.

Singular.

N. *Mi, mise,* I.
G. *Mo,* of me, my.
D. *Dhamh,* to me; *dhamhse,* to me, myself.
A. *Me,* me.
V. ———
A. *Leam,* with me; *uam,* from me; *annam,* in me; *agam,* with, or at me; *assam,* out of, or from me; *dhim,* from off me; *chugam,* to me; *marrium,* with me; *tharum,* over me; *orm,* upon me.

Plural.

N. *Sinn,* we; *sinne,* we ourselves; *(nosmet.)*
G. *Ar,* of us, our. It has *ne* added to the according substantive; as, *ar cretoira-ne,* &c.
D. *Dhuin, dhuine,* to us.
A. *Sinn, sinne,* us.
V. ———
A. *Lein, leinne,* with us; *uain, uaine,* from us; *annin, annine,* in us; *agin, aginne,* with us, in our possession; *assin, assine,* out of, or from us; *dhinne,* from off us: *chugin,* to us; *marrin,* with us; *tharin,* over us.

Note, that *fein* and *se,* when added to the simple pronoun or substantive, are equivalent to the Latin *met, metipsos,* the French *propre,* or English *self, selves;* as, *mo lamh-sa,* my hand; *mo lamh fein,* my own hand; *mi fein,* myself.

Singular.

Singular.

N. *Tu*, thou ; *tusa*, thou, thyself.
G. *Do*, of thee, thy.
D. *Dhuit*, to thee.
A. *Thu*, thee.
V. *Thusa!* O thou!
A. *Leat*, with thee ; *uait*, pronounced *vuait*, from thee ; *annad*, in thee ; *agad*, at, or with, or in the possession of thee ; *asad*, out of, or from thee ; *dhiot*, from off thee ; *chugad*, to you ; *marriut*, with you ; *tharad*, over thee ; *ort*, on thee.

Plural.

N. *Sibh, ibh*, ye ; *sibhse, (vosmet.)*
G. *Bhar*, of you, your.
D. *Dhuibh, dhuibhse*, to you.
A. *Sibh, sibhse*, you.
V. *O sibhse!* O ye or you!
A. *Leibh, leibhse*, with you ; *uaibh, uaibhse*, pronounced *vuaibhse*, from you ; *annaibh*, in you ; *agibh*, at, or with, or in the possession of you ; *asibh*, out of you ; *dhibh*, from off you ; *chugibh*, to you ; *marribh*, with you ; *tharibh*, over you.

Singular.

THE GALIC LANGUAGE.

Singular.

N. *E*, or *eisin, i, ise*, he or she.
G. *A, a,* of him, of it, of her, or his, its, her; it writes *se* after its concordant substantive.
D. *Dh'a, dhasan, dhi, dhise,* to him, it, to her.
A. *E, eisin, i, ise,* he, it, her.
V. ——
A. *Leis, leisan, lea, lease,* with him, it, her; *uaidhe, uaiche,* from him, her; *aige, aice,* at, or with, or in the possession of him or her, it; *annsan,* in him, in thee, in it; *inte,* in her, it; *as,* out of him, it; *aisde,* out of her; *dhe, dhi,* from off him, her; *chuige,* to him, it; *chuicca,* to her; *marris,* with him, it; *marria,* with her; *tharis,* over him, it; *thairte,* over her; *air,* on him; *urra,* on her.

Plural.

N. *Iad, iad, idse,* they.
G. *An, an,* their; it writes *se* after the following substantive.
D. *Dhoibh, dhoibh, dhoibhse,* to them.
A. *Iad, iad, iadse,* them.
V. ——
A. *Leo, leosan,* with them; *natha,* from them; *asda,* out of them; *annta,* in them; *ac,* of them; *acca,* at, or with, or in the possession of them; *dhiu,* of them, off them; *chucca,*

to

to them; *marriu*, with them; *tharta*, over them.

Singular.

N. *Co? cia? ciod?* who? which? what?
G. *Cho?* whose?
D. *Co dha?* to whom?
A. *Co?* which? what?
V. ———
A. *Co leis?* with whom, what? whose? *co uaidh?* from whom? *co ann?* in whom, which, what? *co aig?* with whom? or at, or in whose possession? *co dheth?* from off whom?

The Plural is the same.

A, the relative who, that.

N. *A*, who, that.
G. ———
D. *Do a' do*, to which, to whom.
A. *A*, whom, which.
V. ———
A. *Leis a, ler*, with whom, which; *af a*, out of whom, which; *ann a*, in whom, which; *uaidh a*, from whom, which; *aig a*, with whom, at whom, in whose possession: *Uaidh*, I think, might be wrote *o* when it is not joined to the pronoun, as in *uait*; thus, *o an duine*, from the man, is better and easier read than *uadh an duine*.

So, this, is equivalent to *hic* in Latin; and *fin*, he, that, to *ille, iste*, indeclinable. *Ud*, or *òd*, is somewhat relative, and is, in other respects, exactly what *la* is in French, and *there* among cockneys; for we say *an tigh od*, that there house; *cette maison la; egin*, some; *eile*, other; *cheudna*, same; *fa bith*, soever, are put after pronouns and substantives; as, *co fa bith*, whosoever; *duine eile*, another man; *an duine ceudna*, the same man.—*Gach*, every; *gach uile*, contracted *chuile*, all, every, are put before the substantive. *Gach uile* requires the *h* flection in the substantive following; *gach uile dhuine*, every man, all men.

Ti, he, the man who, whosoever, is used thus; *an ti dhiarras gheibh*, he that seeketh shall find.

Though the Prepositions with which *chuige, chuica, chucca*, are compounded, and seem to be of the dative, they, nevertheless, when separate, govern the genitive.

CHAP. IV.

Of Verbs.

VERBS have two Voices, the Active and Passive.—There is scarcely any change of person in either number, that being almost always immediately discovered by the nominal or pronominal nominative following the verb, whether regularly formed, or by the auxiliary verb and the participle; as, *chruinich mi*, I gathered; *chruinich thu*, thou gatheredst; *chruinich e*, he gathered, &c. or *bha mi (ag) cruinuchadh*, I gathered, or was gathering; *bha thu (ag) cruinuchadh*, thou wast gathering, &c.

In a Galic verb, what the Latins call the Gerund or Substantive derived from the verb, is the principal part from which the other tenses are formed and modified.

In the flection or conjugation of a verb, particles, the auxiliary verb *to be*, the aspirate after the initial consonant, and now and then a change of termination, form differently the different tenses. In order to decline a verb, after having the gerund or substantive, or the name of the action before it relates to person, time, or modification, the present participle is formed by putting *ag* before the radix, which always governs the genitive in discourse, and has no change in gender: so from *cruinuchadh*, a collecting or gathering together, is formed *(ag) cruinuchadh*, the present participle. *Ag* is more elegantly written before participles beginning with a vowel; as, *ag iarridh*, seeking.

To form the Infinitive, decline the radix as a substantive, as far as the dative case, which is the infinitive present; there is no other tense of this mood: thus,

thus, *cruinuchadh*, the radix or gerund, fignifies a gathering together, or affembly. The dative of which is *do chruinuchadh*, to gather or affemble. But when the verb begins with a vowel, the infinitive is formed thus; as, *orduchadh*, commanding, ordering; dative, *dh' orduchadh*, the infinitive, to command.

There are two participles perfect: the firft is of fome ufe in the active, but more in the paffive. The one is formed by putting the prepofition *air* inftead of *ag*, as *(ag) cruinuchadh*, affembling; *air cruinuchadh*, affembled. It receives genders thus: For the mafculine it affumes the afpirate *h* and puts *a*, the genitive of the perfon, between it and the prepofition *air*; as, *air a chruinuchadh*, he affembled; Latin, *congregatus*; for the feminine it affumes only the poffeffive pronoun *a*, which is the genitive feminine of *e, i*; as, *air a cruinuchadh*, fhe affembled, *congregata*. The *a*, however, is often loft when the verb begins with a vowel; as, *air orduchadh*, he affembled, for *air a orduchadh*. In the feminine the euphonic *h* is prefixed; as, *air a h orduchadh*.

In difcourfe, this participle governs the genitive of any of the poffeffive pronouns put between the *air* and the verb, and the genitive of a noun when put after it; as, *tha mi air mo threoruchadh*, I am directed; *air treoruchadh an duine*, directed the man. When the dative is put after it, it tranflates the ablative abfolute of the Latins; as, *air treoruchadh dhamh,*

dhamh, I having directed; *air eirachd,* or *eirigh, do'n ghrian,* the fun having rifen.

The other Participle is formed from the radix, by changing its laft fyllable into *te;* thus, *treoruchadh,* directing; *treoruichte,* directed; *cruinuchadh,* affembling together; *cruinichte,* affembled.

The prefent, the paft, and the future tenfes only are formed regularly; but the auxiliary *tha,* I am, in conjunction with the participle, gives rife to the imperfect, perfect definite, and pluperfect.

Though fome fay a language has only as many tenfes as are regularly formed without the auxiliary, yet I am of opinion, a verb cannot be better conjugated than by ftating it in all its different times of action whatfoever; on this account, therefore, in order to afcertain the different ways of fpeaking relative to action in the Galic, and at once to fhew a verb fo arranged into moods and tenfes, by which every poffible difpofition of the Galic verbs, fo various in their moods and tenfes, may be refolved; I am of neceffity obliged to introduce, perhaps, an unufual number of moods.

As the different particles of conjunction and adverb contribute to the variety of moods in this language, I fhall endeavour to fhew the modes of them in feparate claffes. Thefe I will denominatively call, Indicative, Interrogative, Refponfive, Conditional, Negative,

gative, Subjunctive, Optative, Imperative, and Infinitive.

A language modifies a verb so many different ways, either by a change of termination, or the assistance of auxiliaries, and the influence of different particles. The Galic moods are, however, reducible to these:

The Indicative, which at the same time serves as Responsive; and as Conditional, by putting the conditional particles *ma*, if; *nuair*, when; *antra*, when, &c. before it.

The Subjunctive, which, with the particle *an* before it, serves as interrogative, and as the negative, which takes the particle of negation *cho an*, *cho*, or that of the Irish dialect, *ni an*, no, not, before it, and *cho do* before the past tense, and the particles *chum agus go*, to the end that, &c.

The Optative has an imperfect and some past tenses peculiar to itself, with the particle *nach*, *utinam*, I wish that, O that! This mood and its most common tenses may be seen in that most beautiful text, in this language peculiarly pathetic: *O! nach ro iad glic, nach tuigadh iad so, nach cuimhnadh iad an crioch dheirannach.* "O! that they were wise, that they understood this, that they would consider their latter end!" There is also the imperative and the infinitive. The following is an example of a regular verb:

ACTIVE

AN ANALYSIS OF

ACTIVE VOICE.

Indicative Mood.

Comprehending the Responsive and Conditional; the particles of this mood are only the conditional *ma*, if.

Present Tense.

Cruinucham, I assemble.
Cruinuchidh thu, thou assemblest.
Cruinuchidh e, he assembleth.
Cruinuchidh sinn, we assemble.
Cruinuchidh sibh, ye assemble.
Cruinuchidh iad, they assemble.

Or,

Ata, or *tha mi (ag) cruinuchadh,* I am assembling.
Tha thu (ag) cruinuchadh, thou art assembling.
Tha e (ag) cruinuchadh, he is assembling.
Tha sinn (ag) cruinuchadh, we are assembling.
Tha sibh (ag) cruinuchadh, ye are assembling.
Tha iad (ag) cruinuchadh, they are assembling.

Subjunctive Mood.

Comprehending the Interrogative, which prefixes the particle *an;* the Negative, which prefixes *cho, cho an,* or the Irish *ni an, ni* no, not; and other subjunctive particles, *chum agus gu,* to the end that; *ionas gur,* insomuch that; *gu,* that, &c.

Present Tense.

Cruinich mi, I may or can assemble.
Cruinich thu, thou mayest or canst assemble.
Cruinich e, he may or can assemble.
Cruinich sinn, we may or can assemble.
Cruinich sibh, ye may or can assemble.
Cruinich iad, they may or can assemble.

Or,

Bheil mi (ag) cruinuchadh, I may or can be assembling.
Bheil thu (ag) cruinuchadh, thou mayest or canst be assembling.
Bheil e (ag) cruinuchadh, he may or can be assembling.
Bheil sinn (ag) cruinuchadh, we may or can be assembling.
Bheil sibh (ag) cruinuchadh, ye may or can be sembling.
Bheil iad (ag) cruinuchadh, they may or can be assembling.

AN ANALYSIS OF

Indicative Mood continued.

Imperfect.

Bha mi (ag) cruinuchadh, I was assembling.
Bha thu (ag) cruinuchadh, thou wast assembling.
Bha e (ag) cruinuchadh, he was assembling.
Bha sinn (ag) cruinuchadh, we were assembling.
Bha sibh (ag) cruinuchadh, ye were assembling.
Bha iad (ag) cruinuchadh, they were assembling.

Perfect.

Chruinich mi, I assembled.
Chruinich thu, thou assembledst.
Chruinich e, he assembled.
Chruinich sinn, we assembled.
Chruinich sibh, ye assembled.
Chruinich iad, they assembled.

Perfect Definite.

Tha mi air cruinuchadh, I have assembled.
Tha thu air cruinuchadh, thou hast assembled.
Tha e air cruinuchadh, he has assembled.
Tha sinn air cruinuchadh, we have assembled.
Tha sibh air cruinuchadh, ye have assembled.
Tha iad air cruinuchadh, they have assembled.

Subjunctive Mood continued.

Imperfect.

Ro mi (ag) cruinuchadh, I was or have been assembling.
Ro thu (ag) cruinuchadh, thou wast or hast been assembling.
Ro e (ag) cruinuchadh, he was assembling.
Ro sinn (ag) cruinuchadh, we were, or have been assembling.
Ro sibh (ag) cruinuchadh, ye were assembling.
Ro iad (ag) cruinuchadh, they were assembling.

Perfect.

Do *chruinich mi*, I assembled.
Do *chruinich thu*, thou assembledst.
Do *chruinich e*, he assembled.
Do *chruinich sinn*, we assembled.
Do *chruinich sibh*, ye assembled.
Do *chruinich iad*, they assembled.

Perfect Definite.

Bheil mi air cruinuchadh, I have assembled.
Bheil thu air cruinuchadh, thou hast assembled.
Bheil e air cruinuchadh, he has assembled.
Bheil sinn air cruinuchadh, we have assembled.
Bheil sibh air cruinuchadh, ye have assembled.
Bheil iad air cruinuchadh, they have assembled.

Indicative Mood continued.

Pluperfect.

Bha mi air cruinuchadh, I had assembled.
Bha thu air cruinuchadh, thou hadst assembled.
Bha e air cruinuchadh, he had assembled.
Bha sinn air cruinuchadh, we had assembled.
Bha sibh air cruinuchadh, ye had assembled.
Bha iad air cruinuchadh, they had assembled.

Future.

Cruinuchidh mi, I shall or will assemble.
Cruinuchidh thu, thou shalt or wilt assemble.
Cruinuchidh e, he shall or will assemble.
Cruinuchidh sinn, we shall or will assemble.
Cruinuchidh sibh, ye shall or will assemble.
Cruinuchidh iad, they shall or will assemble.

Future Negative, with the Particle *cho*.

Cho *chruinich mi*, I will not assemble.
Cho *chruinich thu*, thou wilt not assemble.
Cho *chruinich e*, he will not assemble.
Cho *chruinich sinn*, we will not assemble.
Cho *chruinich sibh*, ye will not assemble.
Cho *chruinich iad*, they will not assemble.

Subjunctive Mood continued.

Pluperfect.

Ro mi air cruinuchadh, I had assembled.
Ro tu air cruinuchadh, thou hadst assembled.
Ro e air cruinuchadh, he had assembled.
Ro e air cruinuchadh, we had assembled.
Ro sibh air cruinuchadh, ye had assembled.
Ro iad air cruinuchadh, they had assembled.

Future.

Chruinichas mi, I shall have assembled, or shall or will assemble.
Chruinichas thu, thou shalt have assembled.
Chruinichas e, he shall have assembled.
Chruinichas sinn, we shall have assembled.
Chruinichas sibh, ye shall have assembled.
Chruinichas iad, they shall have assembled.

Future Interrogative, with the Particle *an*.

An cruinich mi, shall or will I assemble?
An cruinich thu, shalt or wilt thou assemble?
An cruinich e, shall or will he assemble?
An cruinich sinn, shall or will we assemble?
An cruinich sibh, shall or will ye assemble?
An cruinich iad, shall or will they assemble?

Cruinich

Imperative.

Cruinich, assemble thou.
Cruinichadh e, let him assemble.
Cruinichamid, let us assemble.
Cruinichibh, cruinichibh-se, assemble ye.
Cruinichadh iad, let them assemble.

Infinitive.

Chruinuchadh, to assemble.

Participles.

Pref. *(Ag) cruinuchadh*, assembling.
Perf. *Air cruinuchadh*, assembled.
Fut. *Re cruinuchadh*, about to assemble, assembling.

The Optative Mood has only this Imperfect peculiar to itself.

Chruinichin, I would assemble.
Chruinichadh tu, thou wouldst assemble.
Chruinichadh e, he would assemble.
Chruinichamid, we would assemble.
Chruinichadh sibh, ye would assemble.
Chruinichadh iad, they would assemble.

THE GALIC LANGUAGE 69

The Optative Particles are also put before the
ses of the Subjunctive Mood.

PASSIVE

PASSIVE VOICE.

Indicative Mood.

Present Tense.

Tha mi cruinichte, (or) *air mo cruinuchadh,* I am assembled.
Tha thu cruinichte, (or) *air do cruinuchadh,* thou art assembled.
Tha e, (or) *i, cruinichte,* (or) *air a chruinuchadh,* Masc. *air a cruinuchadh,* Fem. } he is assembled.
Tha sinn cruinichte, (or) *air ar cruinuchadh,* we are assembled.
Tha sibh air bhar cruinuchadh, (or) *cruinichte,* ye are assembled.
Tha iad cruinichte, (or) *air an cruinuchadh,* they are assembled.

Imperfect.

Bha mi cruinichte, (or) *air mo chruinuchadh,* I was assembled.
Bha thu cruinichte, (or) *air do chruinuchadh,* thou wast assembled.
Bha e cruinichte, (or) Masc. *air a chruinuchadh,* (or) Fem. *air a cruinuchadh,* } he was assembled.

Bha

THE GALIC LANGUAGE.

PASSIVE VOICE.

Subjunctive Mood.

Present Tense.

Bheil mi cruinichte, (or) *air mo chruinuchadh,* I am assembled.
Bheil thu cruinichte, (or) *air do chruinuchadh,* thou art assembled.
Bheil e cruinichte, (or) *air a chruinuchadh,* Masc. (or) *air a cruinuchadh,* Fem. } he is assembled.
Bheil sinn cruinichte, (or) *air ar cruinuchadh,* we are assembled.
Bheil sibh cruinichte, (or) *air bhar cruinuchadh,* ye are assembled.
Bheil iad cruinichte, (or) *air au cruinuchadh,* they are assembled.

Imperfect.

Ro mi cruinichte, (or) *air mo chruinuchadh,* I was assembled.
Ro thu air do chruinuchadh, (or) *cruinichte,* thou wast assembled.
Ro e cruinichte, (or) *air a chruinuchadh,* Masc. *air a cruinuchadh,* Fem. } he was assembled.

Indicative Mood continued.

Bha sinn cruinichte, (or) *air ar cruinuchadh*, we were assembled.
Bha sibh cruinichte, (or) *air bhar cruinuchadh*, ye were assembled.
Bha iad cruinichte, (or) *air an cruinuchadh*, they were assembled.

Perfect.

Chruinichadh mi, I was, or have been assembled.
Chruinichadh thu, thou hast been assembled.
Chruinichadh e, he has been assembled.
Chruinichadh sinn, we have been assembled.
Chruinichadh sibh, ye have been assembled.
Chruinichadh iad, they have been assembled.

Future.

Chruinichar mi, I shall or will be assembled.
Chruinichar thu, thou shalt or wilt be assembled.
Chruinichar e, he shall or will be assembled.
Chruinichar sinn, we shall or will be assembled.
Chruinichar sibh, ye shall or will be assembled.
Chruinichar iad, they shall or will be assembled.

Subjunctive Mood continued.

Ro finn cruinichte, (or) *air ar cruinuchadh*, we were assembled.
Ro fibh cruinichte, (or) *air bhar cruinuchadh*, ye were assembled.
Ro iad cruinichte, (or) *air an cruinuchadh*, they were assembled.

Perfect.

Do *chruinichadh mi*, I have been assembled.
Do *chruinichadh thu*, thou haft been assembled.
Do *chruinichadh e*, he has been assembled.
Do *chruinichadh finn*, we have been assembled.
Do *chruinichadh fibh*, ye have been assembled.
Do *chruinichadh iad*, they have been assembled.

Future.

Cruinichar mi, I fhall be assembled.
Cruinichar thu, thou fhalt be assembled.
Cruinichar e, he fhall be assembled.
Cruinichar finn, we fhall be assembled.
Cruinichar fibh, ye fhall be assembled.
Cruinichar iad, they fhall be assembled.

Optative.

Optative.

Imperfect.

Chruinichtadh mi, I would be assembled.
Chruinichtadh thu, thou wouldst be assembled.
Chruinichtadh e, he would be assembled.
Chruinichtamid, we would be assembled.
Chruinichtadh sibh, ye would be assembled.
Chruinichtadh iad, they would be assembled.

Imperative.

Bith cruinichte, be thou assembled.
Bithadh e cruinichte, let him be assembled.
Bithamid cruinichte, let us be assembled.
Bithibh cruinichte, be ye assembled.
Bithadh iad cruinichte, (or) *air an cruinachadh*, let them, &c.

Infinitive.

Pref. *Bhith cruinichte*, (or) *air a chruinuchadh*, to be assembled.

Participle.

Perf. *Cruinichte*, (or) *air a chruinuchadh*, assembled.
Fut. *Re a chruinuchadh*, to be assembled.

The Auxiliary *ata*, (or) *tha*, I am.

Indicative.	Subjunctive.
Present.	Present.
Ata, (or) *tha mi*, I am.	*Bheil mi*, I am.
Tha thu, thou art.	*Bheil thu*, thou art.
Tha e, he is.	*Bheil e*, he is.
Tha sinn, we are.	*Bheil sinn*, we are.
Tha sibh, ye are.	*Bheil sibh*, ye are.
Tha iad, they are.	*Bheil iad*, they are.

The following present is also used, but with this difference, that the former are always followed by adjectives or the participles of verbs; as, *Am bheil thu beartach*, art thou rich? The Indicative answers *tha*, I am; or if negatively, *cho n bheil*, or, *am bheil thu cruinichte*, art thou assembled or met? answer, *tha*, &c. but this is followed by a noun; as, *an tu-se an duine*, art thou the man? the Indicative answers *is mi*; if negatively, *cho mi*, *cho tu*, &c.

Indicative.	Subjunctive.
2d Present.	2d Present.
Is mi, I am.	*Am mi*, am I, is it I?
Is tu, thou art.	*An tu*, art thou? &c.
Is e, he, it, is.	*An e*, is he?
Is sinn, we are.	*An sinn*, are we?
Is sibh, ye are.	*An sibh*, are ye?
Is iad, they are.	*An iad*, are they?

Perfect.

Perfect.   Perfect.

Bha mi, I was, or have been.   *Ro mi*, I was or have been.
Bha thu, thou waſt.   *Ro thu*, thou waſt.
Bha e, he was.   *Ro e*, he was.
Bha ſinn, we were.   *Ro ſinn*, we were.
Bha ſibh, ye were.   *Ro ſibh*, ye were.
Bha iad, they were.   *Ro iad*, they were.

The following 2d Perfect is uſed after the ſame manner as the 2d Preſent Tenſe.

Indicative.   *Subjunctive.*

Bu mi, I was, it was I.   *Bu mi*, I was, was it?
Bu tu, thou waſt, it was you.   *Bu tu*, thou waſt.
B' e, it was he, it was.   *B' e*, he was, was it? w. he?
Bu ſinn, we were.   *Bu ſinn*, we were, wei we?
Bu ſibh, ye were.   *Bu ſibh*, ye were, wei ye?
B' iad, they were.   *B' iad*, they were, wei they?

Future.   Future.

Bithidh mi, I ſhall or will be.   *Bhithas mi*, I ſhall be.
Bithidh thu, thou ſhalt be.   *Bhithas tu*, thou ſhalt be.
Bithidh e, he ſhall be.   *Bhithas e*, he ſhall be.

Bithid

THE GALIC LANGUAGE.

Bithidh finn, we shall be.   *Bhithas finn,* we shall be.
Bithidh sibh, ye shall be.   *Bhithas sibh,* ye shall be.
Bithidh iad, they shall be.   *Bhithas iad,* they shall be.

The Future Negative, with the particle *cho,* not.

The Future Interrogative with the particle *am.*

Cho *bhith mi,* I shall not.   Am *bith mi,* shall I be?
Cho *bhith thu,* thou shalt not be.   Am *bith thu,* shalt thou be?
Cho *bhith e,* he shall not be. Am *bith e,* shall he be?
Cho *bhith finn,* we shall not be.   Am *bith finn,* shall we be?
Cho *bhith sibh,* ye shall not be.   Am *bith sibh,* shall ye be?
Cho *bhith iad,* they shall not be. Am *bith iad,* shall they be?

Optative Imperfect.

Bhithin, I would be.
Bhithadh tu, thou wouldst be.
Bhithadh e, he would be.
Bhithamid, we would be.
Bhithadh sibh, ye would be.
Bhithadh iad, they would be.

Imperative.

Bith thu, be thou.
Bithadh e, let him be.
Bithamid, let us be.

Bithibh,

Bithibh, be ye.
Bithadh iad, let them be.

Infinitive.

Bhith, to be.

Participle.

Perf. *Air bhith*, being, having been.
Fut. *Re bith*, to be, about to be, to come.

Verbs beginning with vowels or diphthongs, or with *f*, have *dh* in the past tenses; as *eisdam*, I hearken; *dh'eisd mi*, I hearkened; with an apostrophe after the *dh'*. In verbs beginning with *f*, however, the *f* is put between the *d* and *h*. The *dh* retains its wonted force and sound; thus, *fosgalam*, I open; *dfhosgal*, I opened, is read as *dh'osgal*.

Example of the First Person of every Tense of a Verb beginning with a vowel.

Ind.	Subj.
Pref. *Orduicham*,	*Orduich mi*.
Tha mi ag orduchadh.	*Bheil mi ag orduchadh*.

Imp.	Opt. Imp.	Imp.
Bha mi ag orduchadh	*Dh'orduichin*.	*Ro mi ag orduchadh*.

Perfect.	Perfect.
Dh'orduich mi.	*D'orduich mi*.

Perf.

Perf. Def.	Perf. Def.
Tha mi air orduchadh.	*Bheil mi ar orduchadh.*
Plup.	Plup.
Bha mi air orduchadh.	*Ro mi air orduchadh.*
Fut.	Fut.
Orduchidh mi.	*Orduichas mi.*
Fut. Negat.	Fut. Interr.
Cho'n orduich mi.	*An orduich mi.*

Infinitive.

Pref. *Dh'orduchadh.*

Participles.

Pref.   *Ag orduchadh.*
Perf. Act.   *Air orduchadh.*
Fut.   *Re orduchadh.*

Imperative.

Orduich, orduichadh e.
Orduichamid, orduichibh.
Orduichadh iad.

Examples of Irregular Verbs.

Indicative.	*Subjunctive.*
Prefent.	Prefent.
Feudam, I am able.	*Feud mi,* I am able.
Feudidh thu, thou art able.	*Feud thu,* thou art able.
	Feudidh

Indicative	Subjunctive
Feudidh e, he is able.	*Feud e*, he is able.
Feudidh sinn, we are able.	*Feud sinn*, we are able.
Feudidh sibh, ye are able.	*Feud sibh*, ye are able.
Feudidh iad, they are able.	*Feud iad*, they are able.

Indicative.

Past.

Dfheud mi, I was able.
Dfheud thu, thou wast able.
Dfheud e, he was able.
Dfheud sinn, we were able.
Dfheud sibh, ye were able.
Dfheud iad, they were able.

Subjunctive.

Past.

D'fheud mi, I was able.
D'fheud thu, thou wast able.
D'fheud e, he was able.
D'fheud sinn, we were able.
D'fheud sibh, ye were able.
D'fheud iad, they were able.

Future.

Feudidh mi, I shall be able.
Feudidh thu, thou shalt be able.
Feudidh e, he shall be able.
Feudidh sinn, we shall be able.
Feudidh sibh, ye shall be able.
Feudidh iad, they shall be able.

Future.

Dfheudas mi, I shall be able.
Dfheudas thu, thou shalt be able.
Dfheudas e, he shall be able.
Dfheudas sinn, we shall be able.
Dfheudas sibh, ye shall be able.
Dfheudas iad, they shall be able.

Optative.

Optative.

Imperfect.

Dfheudin, I might or could.
Dfheudadh tu, thou couldft.
Dfheudadh e, he could.
Dfheudamid, we might or could.
Dfheudadh fibh, ye might or could.
Dfheudadh iad, they might or could.

[The reft of the Tenfes wanting.]

Indicative.	*Subjunctive.*
Prefent.	Prefent.
Deanam, I do or make.	*Dean mi*, I do.
Deanidh thu, thou doft.	*Dean thu*, thou doft.
Deanidh e, he doth.	*Dean e*, he doth.
Deanidh finn, we do.	*Dean finn*, we do.
Deanidh fibh, ye do.	*Dean fibh*, ye do.
Deanidh iad, they do.	*Dean iad*, they do.
Perf. Def.	Perf. Def.
Bha mi air deanamh.	*Ro thu air deanamh.*
Paft.	Paft.
Rinn mi, I have done.	Do *rinn mi*, I have done.
Rinn thu, thou haft done.	Do *rinn thu*, thou haft done.
Rinn e, he hath done.	
Rinn finn, we have done.	Do *rinn e*, he hath done.

L *Rinn*

AN ANALYSIS OF

Rinn sibh, ye have done.
Rinn iad, they have done.

Do *rinn sinn*, we have done.
Do *rinn sibh*, ye have done.
Do *rinn iad*, they have done.

Future.

Deanidh, (or) *ni mi*, I shall do.
Deanidh, (or) *ni thu*, thou shalt do.
Deanidh, (or) *ni e*, he shall do.
Deanidh, ni sinn, we shall do.
Deanidh, ni sibh, ye shall do.
Deanidh, ni iad, they shall do.

Future.

Dheanas mi, I shall do.
Dheanas thu, thou shalt do.
Dheanas e, he shall do.
Dheanas sinn, we shall do.
Dheanas sibh, ye shall do.
Dheanas iad, they shall do.

Optative.

Imperfect.

Dheanin, I would make.
Dheanadh tu, thou wouldst make.
Dheanadh e, he would make.
Dheanamid, we would make.
Dheanadh sibh, ye would make.
Dheanadh iad, they would make.

Imperative.

Imperative.

Dean, do thou.
Deanadh e, let him do.
Deanamid, let us do.
Deanibh, do ye.
Deanadh iad, let them do.

Infinitive.

Present. *Dheanadh, Dheanamh*, to do.

Participles.

Present.   *(Ag) deanamh*, doing.
Perf. Act. *Air deanamh*, having done.
Future.   *Re deanamh*, about to do.

PASSIVE.

Indicative.   *Subjunctive.*

Present.   Present.

Tha mi deante, I am made.   *Bheil mi deante*, I am made.
Tha thu deante, thou art made.   *Bheil thu deante*, thou art made.
Tha e deante, he is made.   *Bheil e deante*, he is made.

Tha finn deante, we are made.
Tha fibh deante, ye are made.
Tha iad deante, (or) *air an deanamh*, they are made.

Bheil finn deante, we are made.
Bheil fibh deante, ye are made.
Bheil iad deante, (or) *air an deanamh*, they are made.

Imperfect.

Bha mi deante, I was made.
Bha thu deante, thou waſt made.
Bha e deante, he was made.
Bha finn deante, we were made.
Bha fibh deante, ye were made.
Bha iad deante, (or) *air an deanamh*, they were made.

Imperfect.

Ro mi deante, I was made.
Ro thu deante, thou waſt made.
Ro e deante, he was made.
Ro finn deante, we were made.
Ro fibh deante, ye were made.
Ro iad deante, (or) *air an deanamh*, they were made.

Perfect.

Rinnadh mi, I was made.
Rinnadh thu, thou waſt made.
Rinnadh e, he was made.
Rinnadh finn, we were made.
Rinnadh fibh, ye were made.

Perfect.

Do rinnadh mi, I was made.
Do rinnadh thu, thou waſt made.
Do rinnadh e, he was made.
Do rinnadh finn, we were made.
Do rinnadh fibh, ye were made.

Rinnadh iad, they were made.   *Do rinnadh iad,* they were made.

   Future.   Future.

Nitar mi, I shall be made. *Deantar mi,* I shall be made.
Nitar thu, thou shalt be made. *Deantar thu,* thou shalt be made.
Nitar e, he shall be made. *Deantar e,* he shall be made.
Nitar sinn, we shall be made. *Deantar sinn,* we shall be made.
Nitar sibh, ye shall be made. *Deantar sibh,* ye shall be made.
Nitar iad, they shall be made. *Deantar iad,* they shall be made.

     Imperative.

Bith deante, (or) *air do dheanamh,* be thou made.
Bithadh e deante, let him be made.
Bithamid deante, let us be made.
Bithibh deante, be ye made.
Bithadh iad deante, let them be made.

     Infinitive.

Bhith deante, (or) *air a dheanamh,* to be made.

     Participles.

Perfect. *Deante,* (or) *air a dheanamh,* done.
Future. *Re a dheanamh,* to be done.

           Optative.

Optative.

Imperfect.

Dheantadh mi, I would be done.
Dheantadh thu, thou wouldst be done.
Dheantadh e, he would be done.
Dheantadh sinn, we would be done.
Dheantadh sibh, ye would be done.
Dheantadh iad, they would be done.

Indicative.	Subjunctive.
Present.	Present.
Racham, I go; or, *tha mi (ag) dol,* I am going.	*Bheil mi (ag) dol,* I am going.
Imperfect.	Imperfect.
Bha mi (ag) dol, I was going.	*Ro mi (ag) dol,* I was going.
Perfect.	Perfect.
Chuaidh mi, I went.	*Do chuaidh mi, (deachidh),* I went.
Perfect Def.	Perfect Def.
Tha mi air dol, I have gone.	*Bheil mi air dol,* I have gone.
	Pluperfect.

THE GALIC LANGUAGE.

Pluperfect.   Pluperfect.
Bha mi air dol, I had gone.   *Ro mi air dol,* I had gone.

Future.   Future.
Theid mi, I will go.   An *d'theid mi,* I will go.

Optative.

Imperfect.
Rachin, I would go.

Infinitive.
Present.   *Dhol,* to go.

Participles.
Present.   *(Ag) dol.*
Perfect.   *Air dol,* having gone, gone.
Future.   *Re dol,* about to go.

Indicative.   Subjunctive.

Present.   Present.

Tigam, (or) *tha mi teachd,*   *Bheil mi teachd,* I come.
   I come, am coming.

Imperfect.   Imperfect.
Bha mi teachd, I was com-   *Ro mi teachd,* I was coming.   ing.

Perfect.   Perfect.
Thanic mi, I came.   *D'thanic mi,* I came.
                      Perfect.

Perf. Def.	Perf. Def.
Tha mi air teachd, I have come.	*Bheil mi air teachd*, I have come.
Pluperfect.	Pluperfect.
Bha mi air teachd, I had come.	*Ro mi air teachd*, I had come.
Future.	Future.
Thig mi, I will come.	*Tig mi*, I will come.

Imperative.

Thig, come thou.
Thigadh e, let him come.
Thigamid, let us come.
Thigibh, come ye.
Thigadh iad, let them come.

Infinitive.

Theachd, to come.

Participles.

Prefent. *(Ag) teachd*, coming.
Perfect. *Air teachd*, come, having come.
Future. *Re teachd*, about to come.

Optative.

Imperfect.

Thigin, I would come.

Indicative.

Indicative.   *Subjunctive.*

Present.   Present.

Deiram, I say, (or) *tha mi (ag) radh,* I am saying.   *Abeir mi,* I say, (or) *bheil mi (ag) radh,* I am saying.

Imperfect.

Bha mi (ag) radh, I was saying.   *Ro mi (ag) radh,* I was saying.

Past.

Thuairt mi, I said, or have said.   *Duairt mi,* I said, (in Irish) *dubhairt.*

Future.

Their mi, I will say.   *Abeir,* shall I say.

Optative.

Indicatively and Responsively.   *Interrogatively and Negatively.*

Imperfect.   Imperfect.

Theirin, I would say.   *Abrain,* would I say?

Imperative.

Abeir, say thou; *abradh e,* let him say; *abramid,* let us say; *abribh,* say ye; *abradh iad,* let them say.

M   *Participles.*

Participles.

Present. *(Ag) radh,* saying.
Perfect. *Air a radh,* said.
Future. *Re a radh,* to be said.

The Passive has only the Future, which is commonly used impersonally.

Indicative.	*Subjunctive.*
Their ar, shall be said.	*Abrair,* shall be said.

The three last Irregular Verbs have also an Imperfect Optative, used likewise impersonally.

Indicative.	*Subjunctive.*
Rachtadh, would be gone.	*Rachtadh,* would be gone.
Thigtadh, would be come.	*Tigtadh,* would be gone.
Theirtadh, would be said.	*Abeirtadh,* would be said.

Bheiram, I give.   *Toir mi,* I give.

Or,

Tha mi toirt, I am giving.   *Bheil mi toirt,* I am giving.

Imperfect.

Bha mi toirt, I was giving.   *Ro mi toirt,* I was giving.

Perfect.

Thug mi, I gave.   *D' thug mi,* I gave.

Perfect

Perfect Definite.

Tha mi air toirt, I have given.   *Bheil mi air toirt,* I have given.

Pluperfect.

Bha mi air toirt, I had given.   *Ro mi air toirt,* I had given.

Future.

Bheir mi, I shall give.   *Toir mi?* shall I give?

Imperative.

Thoir, give thou; *thugadh e,* let him give; *thugamid,* let us give; *thugibh,* give ye; *thugadh iad,* let them give.

Infinitive.

Thoirt, to give.

Participles.

Present. *Toirt,* giving.
Perfect. *Air toirt,* having given, given.
Future. *Re toirt,* about to give.

Optative.

Indicative.   Subjunctive.
Bherin, I would give.   *Tugin,* I would give.

PASSIVE.

PASSIVE.

Indicative. *Subjunctive.*

Present. Present.
Tha mi air mo thoirt, I *Bheil mi air mo thoirt,* I
  am given.   am given.

Imperfect.
Bha mi air mo thoirt, I *Ro mi air mo thoirt,* I
  was given.   was given.

Perfect.
Thugadh mi, I was given. *D' thugadh mi,* I was given.

Future.
Bheirar mi, I shall be *Toirar mi,* I shall be
  given.   given.

[Imperative wanting.]

Infinitive.
Bhith air a thoirt, to be given.

Participles.
Perfect. *Air a thoirt,* given.
Future. *Re a thoirt,* to be given.

Optative.
Imperfect.
Thugtadh mi, I would be *D' thugtadh mi,* I would
  given.   be given.

Remarks

Remarks on the Verbs.

The adverbs *antra, nuair,* when; *ma,* if; are joined with the past tenses of the Indicative, but always with the Subjunctive; thus, *nuair chruinich iad clocha,* when they gathered stones together; with the Subjunctive, *nuair ghabhas iad comhnuidh,* when they shall rest.

The adverbs *cho,* not; *cho do,* not; *an,* the interrogative particle; the conjunctions *chum agus gu,* so that; *ionas gur,* insomuch that; *chionn nach,* because not; *bhri nach,* because not; *nach,* not; are used also interrogatively; was not? would that? and are always put before the Subjunctive mood; so, *cho chruinich iad na clocha,* they will not gather the stones. *Chum agus gu ro iad air an cruinuchadh,* (or) *cruinichte,* so that they were assembled, or gathered together. *Chionn nach ro iad cruinichte,* because they were not gathered together. *Nach* is an optative particle; thus, *O nach cruinuchadh iad!* O that they would assemble!

Ag, the sign of the participle present, is not always written before the verbs beginning with consonants; as, *tha mi smuintuchadh,* I am considering; in place of *tha mi ag smuointuchadh.* In poetry it is used or neglected as best suits the poet; but before participles beginning with a vowel, it is indispensable; as, *bha iad*

iad ag imthachd, they were departing. When the last word before *ag* ends with a vowel, and the participle begins with a vowel, the *g* only is retained; thus, *bha mi'g eisdachd*, I was listening.

CHAP. V.

Adverbs.

Cait? where?
Annso, here.
Annsin, there, then.
Amach, out.
Anois, now.
Nois, now.
Andiugh, to-day.
Anochd, to-night.
Ande, yesterday.
Anroir, yesternight.
Far? where?
Cia mar, cionas, how.
Cia-fhad agus, as long as.
O chion fad, long since.
Am fad agus, whilst.
Ni, not; *na*, not.
Neamh, best orthographied, *neo*, a negative particle, compounded with nouns.
Ath signifies again, answering to the Latin *re*, compounded with verbs.
Ain, a negative particle, compounded with adjectives.
Treis, greis, a while.
Tammull, a short space, a minute.
Coid airson? for what? why?
Air tus, first, first place.
Ath-ait, dara ait, 2d place.
An treas ait, the 3d place.
An ceathro ait, the 4th place.
An cuigo ait, the 5th place.
Anuairith, last year.
Am marach, to-morrow.

Anns an mhaiddin, in the morning.
Anns an fheasgar, in the evening.
Roi, before.
Roi so, before now.
Roi an de, before yesterday.
Roi an diugh, before to-day.
Riamh, ever.
An la roi, the day before, t' other day.
Fos, fosd, yet, still.
An nearthrath, day after to-morrow.
O chionn ghairrid, lately, presently.
Gan mboil, gan stad, immediately.
Annamh, seldom.
Tric, often.
Air uaire, at times.
Aris, again.
Air ais, back.
Do ghna, pronounced *do ghra*, always.
Go tric, often; *go minic*, often.
Co tric, as often; *co tric agus*, as oft as.

Aon uair, once.
Da uair, twice; *tri uaire*, thrice.
Ann a dheidh sin, afterwards, after these things.
Tuile fos, moreover.
Mar sin, so, in that manner.
Cia uime, cia air son? why? for what?
Ma seach, one by one.
Ann ceart uair, ann cais, just now, directly.
Uair egin, some time or other.
An ath la, the next day.
Feadh, whilst.
Foi chean da la, in two days.
Am feasd, never.
Go sioruidh, for ever.
Cuine, when.
Re an la, the whole day.
Riamh, ever, at any time.
Idir, at all.
Amhuil, thus, in this manner.
Amhli, as, just as.
Amhain, only.
O so suas, henceforth.
Agus mar sin sios, and so forth, et cetera.

Chuile

Chuile la, gach la, every day.
Ni's mo, no more.
Uair eile, another time.
Anns a' cheart am, in the mean time.
Fa leath, separately, one by one.
Ach beg, cho mhor, almost.
Go brach, for ever.
O la gu la, from day to day, day by day.
O am gu am, from time to time.
Go leir, altogether.
Go leoir, enough.
Ro, very, too.
Ioma uair, often, many a time.
Marſo, this way.
Anios, up.
Sios, down.
Anuas, down.
Suas, up.
Bhos, here below.
Annſud & annſo, here and there.
Shios & ſhuas, above and below.
Oſcion & foa, over and beneath.
Mancuairt, round about.
Cia mead? how many?
Am fad, far.
Am fad & am foguſg, far and near.
O chian, formerly, in the days of yore.
Mar gu, as if.
Coi-lion, as many as.
Reradh, indeed, in truth.
Mu'n, before that.
Le cheile, together.
Na, than.
Roi a cheile, feadh a cheile, confuſedly.
Air egin, ſcarcely.
Uidh air uidh, by degrees, ſtep by ſtep.

CHAP.

CHAP. VI.

Prepositions.

PREPOSITIONS, in discourse, govern either the Genitive, Dative, or the Ablative.

Prepositions governing the Genitive.

Air toisach, before.
Ann aghai, against, in the face of.
Tiomchiol, about.
Chum, unto.
Air feadh, among.
Am measg, among.
Airson, for, for the sake of.
Ann lamh, in the possession of.
Do thaobh, concerning.
Anndeigh, after.
Air cul, behind.
Reir, according to.
Oscion, above.
Ann coinamh, over against, opposite.
Anncois, nigh to.
Re cois, nigh to.
Trid, by, through.
Ionsuidh, unto.

Prepositions governing the Dative.

Do, sometimes *dh'* before nouns beginning with a vowel, to, out of.
Air an taobh so, on this side.
Dlu, nigh.
Air an taobh eile, on the other side.
Thall, beyond.

Taobh amach, the outside, without.
Gan fhios, without the knowledge of.
Ri, ris, unto, to.

Amach, out, without.
Mach, out.
Mach as, out of.
O, from, off.

Prepositions governing the Ablative.

Aig, at, in the hands or possession of.
Gu, gus, unto.
As, amach, out, out of.
Foi, under.
Thar, tharis, over.

Lamh ri, ris, nigh to.
Le, leis, with.
Ann, in.
Uaidh, rather *o*, from.
Gan, without.
Air, upon.

Prepositions governing the Accusative or Ablative.

Eidar, between.
Gu, unto.
Gan, without.

Suas, up.
Anuas, down.

CHAP.

CHAP. VII.

Interjections.

INTERJECTIONS are common to the Galic with all other languages. Whatever changes may happen to languages, this part is always secure, and will continue the same whilst the feelings, the sighs, and the groans of the Philosopher and the Savage are alike. These sounds, if not articulations, seem little different from those of the brutes. They are the efforts of Nature to relieve itself in certain cases. They are the fewest words in any language, and on which Grammarians have always had least to say. They express

Laughter, as, *ah! ah! ah! ah!*
Grief, *och! och! mo chreach!* my ruin! *mo thruaidh!* my misery!
Derision, as, *hah! aha! mo nair ort!* fy on you!
Fatigue, as, *heich ho!*
Admiration, as, *oh! ho!*
Imprecation, *mulachd dho*, pox on't!
Demonstration, *feuch!* behold!
Terror, *chugibh! chugibh!*

CHAP. VIII.

Conjunctions.

Agus, and; better contracted '*us* than '*is*, to distinguish it from the substantive verb *is*.
Araon, both.
Uimesin, wherefore.
Air an abhar sin, therefore.
Cuideachd, likewise, also.
Fos, also.
Ge, though.
Giodheadh, however, notwithstanding.
Ma, if.
Ach, but.
An, the Interrogative Particle, changed (like the article) into *am* before *b, f, p*.
Nach, no, O that!
Eadhon, namely, that is to say, viz. i. e.
Gu, that, changed into *gur* before words beginning with a vowel, and the consonants *f, b, p, f, m, n*.
Chum agus gu, to the end that.
Ionas gur, so that.
Na, than.
Mun am, mun an, if not; *mur*, if not.

CHAP. IX.

Of the Formation of the Parts of Speech.

AFTER considering the various inflections of the parts of speech, it is natural to enquire into their formation. Ideas vary with things, and the names of things with ideas. The formative nouns are Diminutives, Collectives, Abstracts, Agents, and Actions.

1. *Of Diminutives.*

All Diminutives of the feminine gender in this language end in *og* or *ag;* those of the masculine in *an,* by subjoining these syllables; as, *nian,* a girl; *nianag,* a little girl; *caillach,* an old woman; *caillachag,* a little old woman: *sguab,* a sheaf; *sguabag,* a little sheaf: *leanabh,* a child; *leanaban,* a little child: *duine,* a man; *duinan,* a little man, a mannikin, *homunculus.* Few or none of the christian names are diminutive.

2. *Of Collectives.*

Collective nouns are not confined to any termination. Among many the following may be reckoned:

Au Fheine, the Fingalians, or followers and army of Fingal, king of Morven, and hero of Ossian's Poems. *Fine*, a nation or tribe; *clann*, a clan or family, the followers and descendants of a Baron or Chieftain, literally children; *crodh*, cattle; *pobul*, people; *buidhan*, a band; *compailt*, company; *uaisle*, gentry.

3. *Of Abstracts.*

Most of the Galic abstracts terminate in *achd* or *as*. *Achd* is generally a feminine termination.

Some adjectives in *achd* add *as* for their abstract; as, *gairdach*, joyful; *gairdachas*, joyfulness: *miobhuidhach*, ungrateful; *miobhuidhachas*, ungratefulness: *dubhach*, sad; *dubhachas*, sadness. Some change the *ach* into *as*; as, *beartach*, rich; *beartas*, riches: *fiuntach*, generous; *fiuntas*, generosity: *athreach*, penitent; *athreachas*, penitence.

Some substantives and adjectives which have *i* in their last syllable, have *as* rather than *achd* sometimes added; or the termination changed to *as*; so, *cruaidh*, hard; *cruas*, hardness: *carid*, a friend; *cairdas*, friendship: *fuairc*, gentle; *fuaircas*, gentleness: *math*, good; *mathas*, goodness: *cliamhin*, a kinsman; *cleamhnas*, affinity: *udar*, an author; *udaras*, authority: *neo-ghlioc*, imprudent; *neo-ghliocas*, imprudence: *sona*, happy; *sonas*, happiness.

Those

Those in *ol* or *al* prefer *achd*; as, *furdol*, industrious; *furdolachd*, industry; *froal*, prodigal; *froalachd*, prodigality: *neothaincol*, unthankful; *neothaincolachd*, unthankfulness: *cuirtal*, courtly; *cuirtalachd*, courtliness, courtesy; *cairdol*, friendly; *cairdolachd*, friendliness: *aidhol*, hospitable; *aidholachd*, hospitality: *coinol*, kind; *coinolachd*, kindness, clemency: *moral*, magnificent; *moralachd*, *morachd*, magnificence, majesty.

Some add *ach*; as, *naomh*, holy; *naomhachd*, holiness: *feamh*, meek; *feamhachd*, meekness: *geamni*, chaste; *geamniachd*, chastity: *iriofal*, humble; *iriofachd*, humility. All, likewise, that end in *or* or *mhor*, add *achd*; as, *ceolor*, musical; *ceolorachd*: *mor*, great; *morachd*, majesty, greatness: *feolor*, sensual; *feolorachd*, sensuality.

The irregular adjectives form the following abstracts; *lugha*, less; *lughad*, littleness, smallness: *moa*, greater; *mead*, greatness: *leatha*, broader; *lead*, breadth; *airde*, higher; *airde*, height: *olc*, bad; *olcas*, badness; *giurra*, shorter; *giurrad*, shortness.

4. *Of Actions.*

Actions are the verbal nouns, derived from verbs, or the present participle of a verb; thus, *cruinuchadh* is, at the same time, the participle and the verbal noun. They generally end in *adh*; as, *fiofruchadh*, knowledge,

knowledge, or judgment, from *fiosrucham*, to judge or enquire into; *iriosluchadh*, humiliation, from *irioslucham*, I humble; *mifnuchadh*, encouragement, from *mifnucham*, I encourage: *meadachadh*, multiplying or encreasing, from *meaducham*, I encrease or multiply.

Some end in *in*; as, *faicsin*, from *faicam*, I see; *cluintin*, hearing, from *cluinam*, I hear; *teasargain*, deliverance, from *teasargam*, I deliver. Some end in *achd*; as, *cantairachd*, an hymning or singing, from *canam*, I sing; *mosgaltachd*, vigilance, from *mosgalam*, I wake or watch.

5. *Of Agents.*

Agents or doers subjoin *oir*, and sometimes *air*, to the present participle of verbs; as, *scriobhadh*, writing; *scriobhadoir*, a writer or attorney: *tagradh*, a pursuing or process; *tagradair*, or *fear tagraidh*, a prosecutor: or by changing the termination into *air*; as, *Cruthichoir*, the Creator, from *cruthuchadh*, a creating.

Some write the termination *fhear* in place of *oir*, affecting an idle knowledge in the etymology of words, at the expence of hurting the eye of every reader with the bristly appearance of an useless assemblage of consonants. No more consonants than are necessary to express the true pronunciation of words ought to be written; and since the number of diphthongs

diphthongs and triphthongs are ascertained (as attempted in this Analysis), many of the consonants formerly written become superfluous. It would be as just in Latin to write *amatvir* instead of *amator*, as to write in Galic *flanuigh fheair* in place of *flanivir*.

Some are formed by adding *ich*; as, *buain*, reaping; *buanich*, a reaper; *fnamh*, swimming; *fnamhich*, a swimmer.

Others are formed by making the name *fearr*, a man, or *bean*, a woman, govern the action in the genitive; as, *fear-tighe*, an husbandman; *bean-tighe*, an housewife: *fear-ceaird*, a mechanic; *fear-baile*, a freeholder, a laird, sometimes a tacksman or lessee; *fear-bainse*, a bridegroom; *bean-bainse*, a bride; *fear-moirt*, a murderer; *riogh*, a king; *bean-riogh*, a queen; *diuc*, a duke; *bean-diuc*, a duchess; *priunse*, a prince; *bean-phriunse*, a princess; *iarla*, an earl, *bean-iarla*, a countess; *baran*, a baron, *bean-bharain*, a baroness; *morair*, a lord, or great man; *bean-morair*, a great lady: *tiarna*, a general name for a proprietor or lord over any thing, commonly an esquire, has *bean-tiarna*, applied to gentlewomen in general, as the English word Lady.

Some are also formed by making the collective words *luchg*, or *muintir*, govern the action in the genitive; as, *luchg faire*, watchmen; *luchg fairg*, seamen; *luchg feanachais*, historians, &c.

6. *Of Adjectives.*

All Collectives end in *ach*, *agach*, or *anach*, terminations equal to *osus* in Latin; thus, *ballach*, spotted, full of spots, is formed from *ball*, a spot; *bainach*, milky, from *baine*; *badanach*, full of locks; *cathach*, of or belonging to battles, from *cath*, a battle; *griannach*, sunny, from *grian*, the sun.

Those which signify tendency end in *ol*; so, *feimol*, necessary, from *feim*, use, necessity; *laichol*, daily, from *la*, a day; *coinol*, kindly, from *coinas*; *froal*, prodigal, from *fro*, prodigality; *misnachol*, courageous, from *misnach*, courage; *gaisgol*, valiant, from *gaisge*, valour; *ainmol*, renowned, from *ainm*, a name.

Those that subjoin *or* to the primitive, signify *abounding in, full of*; as, *sultor*, full of sap, from *sult*, fat; *Trenmore*, a man of strength and valour, one of Ossian's heroes; *tlachdor*, handsome, from *tlachd*, a liking, handsomeness; *ceolor*, in the Irish dialect *ceolmhor*, musical, eminent in music, from *ceol*, music; *Cathmor*, great in battle, one of Ossian's heroes, from *cath*, a battle.

All gentile or patronymic Adjectives end in *ach*; as *Albanach*, a Scotsman; *Erinach*, an Hibernian; *Sasganach*, an Englishman; *Francach*, a Frenchman; *Fedaltach*, an Italian; *Lochlunach*, a Dane.

Adjectives that shew possibility and facility prefix *so*; as, *so thuigse*, easy to be understood, intelligible; *so thogal*, easy to be lifted up or acquired; *so dheante*, easy to be done, possible. Those that denote impossibility prefix *do*; as, *do-thuigse*, difficult to understand, unintelligible; *do-thogal*, not easily taken up or acquired; *do-dheante*, that cannot be done, impossible.

7. *Of Numerals.*

Aon and *da*, one, two, have the aspirate *h* after the initial consonant of the noun agreeing with it, and which in discourse always come after. All others agree with it; thus we say *aon fhear*, one man; *da fhear*, two men; but we say *tri fir*, three men; *ceithar fir*, four men, &c. as far as *aon deug*, eleven, and then we go on as before, *aon fhear deug*, *da fhear deug*, but we say *tri fir deug*, &c. always putting *deug* after the substantive.

The substantive always stands between the unit and the ten, when the substantive must agree with the unit; thus, *aon fhear*, one man; *da fhear*, two men; *aon fhear deug*, eleven men; *da fhear deug*, twelve men; *tri fir deug*, thirteen, &c.

Cardinals.

Aon, one.
Da, dis, two, the two.
Tri, three.
Ceithar, four.

Coig,

Coig, five.
Sia, six.
Seachd, seven.
Ochd, eight.
Noi, nine.
Deich, ten.
Aon deug, eleven.
Da dheug, twelve.
Tri deug, thirteen.
Ceithar deug, fourteen.
Coig deug, fifteen.
Sia deug, sixteen.
Seachd deug, seventeen.
Ochd deug, eighteen.
Noi deug, nineteen.
Fichid, twenty.
Aon thar fichid, twenty-one.
Deich thar fichid, thirty.
Aon deug thar fichid, thirty-one, &c.
Da fhichid, forty.
Aon agus da fhichid, forty-one.
Deich & da fhichid, fifty.
Aon deug & da fhichid, fifty-one.
Tri fichid, sixty.
Aon & tri fichid, sixty-one.
Deich & tri fichid, seventy.
Aon deug & tri fichid, seventy-one, &c.
Ceithar fichid, eighty.
Aon & ceithar fichid, eighty-one.
Deich & ceithar fichid, ninety.
Aon deug & ceithar fichid, ninety-one.
Coig fichid, or *ciad*, an hundred.
Da chiad, two hundred.
Mille, deich chiad, a thousand.

Triochad, thirty; *cearachad*, forty; *seasgad*, sixty; *seachdbhad*, seventy; *ochdbhad*, eighty; *nauchad*, ninety, are Irish, and obsolete.

Ordinals,

Ordinals.

An ciad, the first.
An dara, second.
An treas, third.
An ceathro, fourth.
An coigo, fifth.
An siao, sixth.
An seachdo, seventh.
An t ochgo, eighth.
An noio, ninth.
An deicho, tenth.
An t aono deug, eleventh.
An dara deug, twelfth.
An treaso deug, thirteenth.
An ceathro deug, fourteenth.
An ciogo deug, fifteenth.
An siao deug, sixteenth.
An seachgo deug, seventeenth.
An t ochgo deug, eighteenth.
An t noio deug, nineteenth.
An fichido, twentieth.
An t aono thar fhichid, twenty-first.
An deicho thar fhichid, thirtieth.
An t aono deug thar fhichid, thirty-first.
An da fhichido, fortieth.
An t aono thar dha fhichid, forty-first.
An deicho thar dha fhichid, fiftieth.
An t aono deug thar dha fhichid, fifty-first.
An tri fichido, sixtieth.
An t aono thar tri fichid, sixty-first.
An deicho thar tri fichid, seventieth.
At t aono deug thar tri fichid, seventy-first.
An ceithar fichido, eightieth.
An t aono thar ceithar fichid, eighty-first.
An deicho thar ceithar fichid, ninetieth.
An t aono deug thar ceithar fichid, ninety-first.
An coig fichido, or *an ciado*, the hundredth.

Of the Formation of Verbs.

All nouns of action may be conjugated as verbs, without any addition of termination, by observing the flection of the examples already given; as, *eisdachd*, hearing, conjugated *eisdam*, I hear; *mosgladh*, awaking; *mosgalam*, I awake, &c.

Every verb has in the syllable or syllables that compose it, something expressive of its signification, whether rough or smooth, hard or soft, strong or feeble, frequentative or diminutive. These, however, are more commonly expressed in this language by the auxiliary verb, and their vast diversity of adjectives.

The frequentative is expressed as in the participle *leimnach*, often leaping or hopping.

"'S iad a' leimnach o Ossag gu ossag."

Ossian's Temora, Book vii.

Of Adverbs.

Every adjective noun may be converted into an Adverb by prefixing the syllable *go*; thus, *math*, good; *go math*; well; *aidharach*, glad; *go aidharach*, gladly, &c.

CHAP.

CHAP. X.

Of the Composition of the Parts of Speech.

THE richness of a language consists in the number of its primitives, and their capacity of various composition. The original simple principles of the Galic make it far excel any of the modern, and rival the most ancient languages. The little variegated flection of its nouns and verbs, which is peculiar to itself, and the abundance of its compositions, render it capable of beautifully describing and expressing the emotions of the mind, without the aid of foreign words; hence it is, that the illiterate peasant on the hills of Scotland, having, in his infancy, had his mind stored with a certain number of primitives and their different modes of inflection, by an easy, though a various combination with a certain number of particles, speaks his language with elocution, a natural Demosthenes; and there is no word in the language, however compounded, but he understands.

Neither is this language deficient in the terms of art. In Ethics, Jurisprudence, Theology, and Natural History, words are not wanting to express our thoughts, and to instruct others: even in Mathematics, and Natural Philosophy in all its parts, terms can easily be rendered from the Greek into the Galic, by decomposing them in the original, and then trans-
lating

lating and joining them afresh; an advantage of which no modern language is possessed.

Composition is effected in Galic by prefixing the prepositions; as, *neo-impochadh*, unconversion; *an-eolach*, ignorant; or by rightly uniting simple words; as, *grian-stad*, the solstice; *cru-chaochladh*, transfiguration; *ceart-chreidach*, orthodox; *fein-speis*, self-love.

The combinable prepositions are in the Galic inseparable, and are as follow:

Ei, equivalent to the English *not*.
So, equal to the English termination *ble*.
Co, equal to *con* in the Latin.
Ao, equal to *un*.
Ath, again; equal to the Latin *re*.
Mi, un.
Neo, un.
An, very, too; the Latin *per*; as, *an-mhor*, very great; *eidir*, between.

They are thus compounded:

Ei-criona, foolish, unwise.
So-thuigse, intelligible.
Co-chomun, an union of society, a communion.
Ao-dochas, despair.
Ath-nuadhuchadh, a renewing.

Mi-chriodhol, disheartened, discouraged.
Neo-bhasor, immortal.
Eider-theangichte, interpreted.
An-trom, over heavy, (*pergravis*.)

The

THE GALIC LANGUAGE.

The following Substantives may serve as a specimen of Galic nouns compounded:

Geur-chuisach, expert, keen.
Lan-shoilleir, evident.
Buan-mhairachdain, long-liv'd.
Molt-fheoil, mutton.
Mart-fheoil, beef.
Muc-fheoil, pork.
Ceithar-chosach, four-footed.
Ioma-chosach, many-footed.
Gorm-bhreac, mixed with blue.
Geal-lamha, white-handed.
Mala-mhin, meek-eyed.
Cam-shronach, the name Cameron, crook-nosed.
Cam-beulach, Campbell, wry-mouth'd.
Du-glassach, Douglass, dark-grey.
Craobh-sheanachais, genealogical tree.
Treun laoch, an hero.
Gear-ghobach, short-bill'd.
Geur-sgiathach, sharp-winged.
Fuar-bhean, cold mountains.
Binn-foclach, shrill-voiced.
Grian-stad, a solstice.
Marc-shluagh, cavalry.
Taobh-tuath, the north country.
Cliu-thoiltunach, praise-worthy.
Aird-mheamnach, high-minded.
Culidh-bhrostidh, an incentive.
Du-fhocal, a parable.
Fein-fhointach, self-sufficient.
Grian-chrios, the zodiac.
Fa-scriobhadh, an appendix.
Geur-leanbhin, persecution.
Idhol-aoradh, idolatry.
Idhol-aoraidh, an idol.
Nua-bhriouchadh, transubstantiation.

P   *Obair-*

Obair-bharrachd, supere- *Uile-chumhachdach*, Al-
rogation. mighty.

Of compounded Verbs.

All active compounded nouns may be resolved into verbs, and may be conjugated by the examples given, like regular verbs; others are declined by means of the auxiliary; and many verbs which in other languages are compounds, in the Galic have the compositive preposition immediately following the verb; thus, *athnuadhuchadh*, renewing, is the active substantive compounded of *ath* again, and *nuadhuchadh*, making new, is resolved into a verb; thus, *athnuadhicham*, I renew, &c. *dh'athnuadhich mi*, I renewed; *athnuadhuchidh mi*, I shall renew, &c.

In these verbs which admit of the flection *h* after their initial consonants, the same is introduced in both parts of the compounded verb, where the consonants are not immutable. The *n* in the second part of the past tense, *dh'ath-nuadhich*, is immutable, and therefore has no *h*; but in this verb, *athghinam*, I regenerate; *dh'ath-ghin mi*, I regenerated, it is perceptible.

Geur-leanbhin, persecution, is conjugated by the auxiliary; thus, tha mi *geur-leanbhin*, bha mi *geur-liambhin*, &c.

Verbs have some component particles after them,

in

in this manner, *snamham*, I swim; *snamham tharis*, I swim over, acrofs, thus,

" *Mar ghlas-sgiath, roi thaomadh nan nial,*
" *Snamh tharis tha gealach na h oich.*"

OSSIAN.

Of the Adverb in Composition.

As all primitive, fo all compounded adjectives and participles are ufed adverbially, by prefixing the fyllable *go*; thus, *impoichte*, converted; *neo-impoichte*, unconverted; *go neo-impoichte*; *criodhol*, hearty, chearful; *neo-chriodhol*, difheartened, forrowful; *go neo-chriodhol*, forrowfully, in a forrowful manner.

AN

AN ANALYSIS OF THE GALIC LANGUAGE.

BOOK III.

SYNTAX.

SYNTAX is the proper difpofition of words in a language.

General Rules.

I. An adjective and the article agree with a fubftantive in gender, number, and cafe, (the fubftantive always going before the adjective); as, *an* (or) *a' chaoradh bhan,* the white fheep; *an duine bochd,* the poor man.

namhorachd do'n tiarna *na beoil bhreugach*, Prov. xii. 22.

Coimhdidh *bean ghrafor* onoir; agus *fir laidir* faibhras, Prov. xi. 19.

Imich as fianuis *an duine amidaich* nuair nach mothuich thu ann beul an eolais, Prov. xiv. 7.

" *Mhoraig chiataich a' chuil dualaich,*
" Is e do luaidh a tha air m' aire!
Macdonald's Odes.

The poffeffive pronouns *mo*, my; *do*, thy; and the mafculine *a*, his, its; have the *h* afpirate after the initial confonant.

" O Dhia is tu *mo Dhia*, go moch
" Do iarram thu gach la
" Ro thartor ata *m'anam* bochd
" Ann geall ort fein do ghna." Pfal lxiii.

When the noun begins with a vowel the afpirate is loft; as, *m'anam*; *d* in *do*, thy, is changed into *t* before a vowel; as,

O pill rium us dean trocair orm,
Thoir neart do *t' oglach* fein.
Do mhac do bhan-oglaich faraon
Dean fuafgladh ann a fheim.

The poffeffive *a*, his, its, before nouns beginning with vowels, often finks, and is loft. Thus,

Dhoirt

Dhoirt e *anam* amach, he poured out his soul; instead of dhoirt *e a anam*, &c. to shun the hiatus.

In this case, if *a* is the feminine possessive, the *h* euphonic must be introduced; thus, *dhoirt i a h anam amach*, she poured out her soul.

The Irish, and even the Scots, needlessly prefix an *n* to the possessive *a* of either gender; thus, *le na lamh*, with his hand; whilst *e a lamh*, sounds agreeably enough, because the vowels are broad and small.

It is somewhat difficult to know, whether the *a* be masculine or feminine when the noun begins with any of the immutable consonants. The distinction depends on the sense of the sentence; when feminine, the *l, n,* or *r* seems in reading and speaking as if double; thus, *le a lamh*, with his hand; *le a lamh*, with her hand, is pronounced as if *le a llamh*.

As the letter *a* seems to have so many significations, and to serve so many uses, it may be proper here to settle its extent.——The letter *a*, in the modern books in Galic, I believe, has as many different meanings as the *iod* has amongst the Rabinical Doctors of the Jews in their traditions and *Caballa*. Even Mr. Macfarlane, and Mr. Stewart, the translator of the Scotch version of the New Testament, have written this letter of many meanings without any fixed rule. With them and others,

A signifies *his, her*.

A, relative pronoun *that*.

A, for *ag*, the sign of the present participle.

A, sign of the infinitive.

A, a preposition, before the names of places signifies *to*.

A', for *an*, the article *the*.

A, for *O!* a sign of the vocative; as, *a Dhia*, O God!

I leave it to any one who has the least knowledge of grammar, whether it be possible for even those who naturally speak the language, to distinguish the one from the other, where the whole may recur twice or oftener in one page. In order therefore to settle the whole, I have consulted the genius of the language, and dismissed them all except three, which I explain as follows:

A', for *an*, the article used before such nouns of the feminine as begin with particular letters, such as *b, c, p, m*, &c. as, *a' chaoradh*, the sheep; *a' bhiastog*, the worm; *a' bhean*, the woman.

A, the relative pronoun *that*, which has generally its antecedent substantive immediately before it, and which distinguisheth it from

A, the possessive pronoun, *his, her, its*.

First, the relative, and then the possessive, may be seen in the following examples:

Is

Is fonadh an ti *a* gheibh eagnai, agus an duine *a* gheibh tuigse.

Happy is the man that findeth wisdom, and the man that getteth understanding.

Oir is fearr *a* ceannachd na ceannachd airgaid, agus *a* tairbh na or glan.

For the merchandise of it is better than silver, and the gain thereof than fine gold.

II. A verb agrees with its nominative after it immediately; as, *chruinich mi*, I assembled; *scriobh e*, he wrote; *ghlac iad*, they received.

Duisgidh fuath, imreason; ach *folachidh gradh* gach cionta.

Hatred stirreth up strife; but love covereth all sins.

Teasairgidh trocair & *firin* an riogh: agus le trocair cumar suas *a* chathair.

Mercy and truth preserve the king: and his throne is upholden by mercy.

The relative *a*, and the pronoun *an ti*, he, require the aspirate in the verb, though in the present tense; thus,

 An ti chuiras, is e *a bhuainas*.
 He that soweth shall reap.

III. When two substantives come together signifying different things, the latter is put in the genitive; as, *mulach a' chin*, the crown of the head; *bonn na cois*, the sole of the foot; *lamh fir*, a man's head.

Tha *mallachd De* an tigh an droch-dhuine: ach beannuchidh e *aitra an ioraic*.

The curse of the Lord is in the house of the wicked: but he blesseth the habitation of the just. Prov. iii. 33.

Na tig asteach ann *casan nan ciontach*; agus na gluais ann *slighe nan droch-dhaoine*.

Enter not into the path of the wicked; and go not in the way of evil men.

Names of quantity also govern the genitive; as, *moran ionnais*, much treasure; *began sonais*, little good.

IV. Partitives, Superlatives, and Interrogatives govern the Dative, and sometimes the Ablative plural; as, *co agin?* which of us? *aon dhiu*, one of them; *aon is laidre do'n Fheine*, the strongest of the Fingalians.

> *Is onoraiche anois an gniomh,*
> *No coig ceud mile bola;*
> *'S fearr aon siola dsbuil's ann stri*
> *Na Galloinsbion air borda.*
>
> Macdonald's *Odes*.

V. The

V. The measure of any thing has the preposition *air* before the dimension; as, da fhichid traigh *air doimhnachd*, forty feet deep.

VI. Adjectives of plenty and want govern the genitive or dative; thus, *lan fion*, full of wine; *fallamh do thuigse*, void of understanding.

All those Adjectives which signify any affection of the mind have the preposition *air* before the following nouns; thus, *math air fairge*, experienced at sea; *eolach air lagh*, skilled in law, *juris peritus*.

VII. An active verb governs the Accusative; as, *bhuail e me*, he struck me: *scriobh e littir*, he wrote a letter:—*Duisgidh* fuath *imreason:* ach folachidh gradh gach cionta.——Hatred stirreth up strife; but love covereth all sins.——Prov.

N. B. We cannot with strict propriety say that the Galic has an accusative, because the nominative and accusative are always the same. This construction means, that the noun (next to its immediate nominative) following the verb must be of the nominative case. To prove this, *duisgidh imreason* is the verb and nominative, as well as *duisgidh fuath*, only *fuath* is here next the verb: so both are of the nominative; the situation only determining the nominative or person, and the *governed* noun.

EXCEPTION.

EXCEPTION. If the verb be of the infinitive, or of any of the combined tenses, where the participle occurs, the noun following is of the genitive case; as, *dh'eisdachd sgeoil*, to hear news; *ag rusgadh nan craobh*, stripping the trees. And if the word governed be any of the pronouns, it must go before the verb; thus, *Bhraithre ionmhin tha an scrioptoir ag ar brosnuchadh ann iomad ait*, &c.——Dearly beloved brethren, the Scripture moveth us in sundry places, &c.

Here I think it proper to interdict the false constructions common in conversation, and which the Rev. Mr Macfarlane of Killinvir, the only person who seems to have studied the genius of the language, frequently falls into. Instead of writing *ag ar brosnuchadh*, he writes, as it is rapidly pronounced in common speech, *gar brosnuchadh*; nor does he at the same time account for the part of speech *gar*, but leaves it mysterious and undetermined. In like manner *gam*, instead of *ag mo*; as, *ag mo bhuairadh*, disturbing or tempting me; *gam bhuairadh:* so *gam eisdachd*, or *ga m' eisdachd*, in place of *ag m' eisdachd*, hearing me, or listening to me: so likewise *gan*, in place of *ag an;* as, *gan eisdachd*, instead of *ag an eisdachd*. The cause of this mistake, I am certain, is writing from the ear only, without an allowance for the velocity of sound.

VIII. The infinitive (formed by the dative of the present participle) follows a verb of motion; as *chuaidh*

aidh e dhufgadh chlach, he went to raife ftones; or has the noun governed going before it; as, tha e ceart *Dia mholadh*, it is right to praife God: and if an adjective come before it, though at a diftance, the afpirate *h* is dropped, or the nominative of the participle is ufed; thus, Is *egin* dhamh *fcriobhadh*, I muft write; tha mi *deonach dol* amach, I am willing to go out.

IX. The auxiliary verb *ata*, or *tha*, and *is*, with the prepofitions *ag* or *le*, govern the ablative; *tha e agad*, you have it; *is leam e*, it is mine.

X. When a fubftantive comes after the participle perfect of the active voice (made by putting *air* before the prefent), the fubftantive following is put in the dative; as, *air labhairt dhamh*, I having fpoke, or when I fpake. This conftruction is equivalent to the Latin ablative abfolute.

XI. The interjections *O*, and fome others, come before the vocative; as, *O dhuine!* O man!

EXCEPTION. *Anaobhin*, and *mairg*, like the Latin *hei* and *væ*, govern the dative; as, *anaobhin dhuibh*, woe unto you.

XII. The fubjunctive particles *cho*, *cho'n*, *cho do*, not, *chum agus gu*, as obferved under the article of Verb, are joined with the fubjunctive mood. And,

XIII. The

XIII. The conditional particles *ma*, if; *nuair*, when; *antra*, when, &c. before the indicative; examples of which follow:

Subjunctive.	*Indicative.*
An cruinich mise? do, or can, or may I gather?	*Cruinicham,* I gather.
Am bheil thu ag cruinuchadh? art thou gathering?	*Tha mi ag cruinuchadh,* I am gathering.
Cho ro sinn ag cruinuchadh, we were not gathering.	*Bha sinn ag cruinuchadh,* we were gathering.
Chum agus gu do chruinich sibh, so that ye gathered.	*Chruinich sibh,* ye gathered.

XIV. In all languages conjunctions couple like tenses and cases; as, *damsidh thusa us seinidh mise,* you shall dance and I will sing; *a' bhean & na paisdan,* wife and children.

BOOK

AN ANALYSIS OF THE GALIC LANGUAGE.

BOOK IV.

PROSODY.

SOUNDS are either quick or flow, rough or smooth, ftrong or feeble. From the various modifications of thefe in a language, may, perhaps, be difcovered, the manners, the temperament, and feelings of a people, at the time of its formation. The Gael, when their language was formed, feem to have been in that flate of fociety, when the arts of peace and war were not entirely ftrangers; when it was an approved maxim, to " bind the ftrong in " arms, but fpare the feeble hand, be a ftream of " many tides againft the foes of thy people, but like " the gale that moves the grafs to thofe who afk thy " aid."

" aid."—*Parcere subjectis, debellare superbos.* Such was the genius of the language in the days of Trenmor and of Fingal, and even *now* it is the most suited either to rouse the soul to feats of arms, or inspire pity in the relentless breast ;

"To soften rocks, and bend the knotted oak."

" The intermixing of long and short syllables ren-
" ders a language most agreeable. Italian words,
" like those of the Greek and Latin, have this pro-
" perty almost universally, the English and French
" words are generally deficient; in the former the
" long syllable being generally removed from the end
" as far as the sound will permit; and in the latter,
" the last syllable being generally long *." But what renders a language chiefly agreeable, is its power of expressing in sound the nature of the thing signified; this is the true standard to estimate the merit of a language, and tried by which, the Galic will be found inferior to none.

In the Galic certain letters have strong, bold, smooth, or solemn sounds. *O* and *u* are bold, strong, and solemn. The combinations *ai, ei,* are chearful and soft; as *failte!* hail! *compailt,* company; *aighar,* joy. *Ao* is soft and solemn; as, *aoradh,* worship; *aois,* old age. *Eo, io,* are musical; as, *ceol,* music ; *seoladh,* sailing; *iosal,* low.

Consonants likewise have their inherent power of expression.

---

* Elements of Criticism.

expreffion. *L,* and the combinations *bh* and *mh* are soft and meek; as, *liobha,* smooth; *fleamhin,* flippery; *feamh,* mild; *caomh,* meek.——*C* and *g,* with their combinations *ch* and *gh,* are soft, sprightly, and forcible.——*R* is angry and proud; as, *troid,* scolding; *brod,* pride; *ardan,* haughtiness.

All syllables are long or short in their sound; words are made up of one or more syllables; and a sufficient number of words compose a sentence. A sentence, therefore being constituted by words of one or many syllables, or feet, which are long and short, the sentence itself must have many syllables, or feet, long and short. Prose and verse, then, differ only in this, that the first is irregular, and written according to every one's fancy; but the last is always fixed, and subject to rule.

Of Rhime.

No language is more susceptible of Rhime than the Galic; it is not, like the Greek and Latin, chained to certain terminations, which refuse rhime, but at once admits of all the variety of antient and modern versification.

Final rhime in Galic does not confist in terminations of similar letters, but in the last strongly pronounced vowel or dipthong in a word. Thus, *Ceol* and *coir; nan* and *beann; taom, caoin; fioth, fios; tron, trom,* &c. are true rhimes; as,

Inghina Shalem! duifgibh nois an *ceol*
Dh'orana neamhidh 'n guth is aird' is *coir !*
   Neamhidh mar dhriuchd anuas an iocllılant *taom*,
Us ann an geal-fhath fiol an fhras go *caoin !*
   Faic togal fuas a chean ard Leba*non*,
Faic air na cnoic ag damhfadh cranna *trom*.

It has alfo, as well as the Englifh, double rhime.

" You'll find, if once the monarch acts the monk,
" Or, cobler-like, the parfon will get drunk;
" Worth makes the man, and want of it the *fel-
   low*,
" The reft is all but leather or *prunella*.

So,

   Faic neoil lan fpios ag eirachd fuas o *Sharon*,
   Us lus-mhaoth Carmel dea-bholadh nan *Speuran*.

Of Meafure.

The Galic poetry, unlike the Englifh, which is generally confined to diffyllables and monofyllables, admits of words of any length. Galic poets never yet wrote by any other rule than the ear, and certain pieces of mufic; and for that reafon, though we may eafily fee what fort of meafure each piece delights in, the uniformity of the fame number of fimilar meafures in every line, does not always return. This may be eafily accounted for, by obferv-
ing,

ing, that all compositions have hitherto been orally repeated, and which, by different persons, will ever be differently performed: whereas, had these pieces been written, every one would have repeated them alike. Even Ossian's poem could not be scanned; for every reciting bard pronounced some words differently, and sometimes substituted one for another. Nevertheless, the poetry always pleases the ear, and is well adapted to the music for which it was originally intended; and the language and composition seldom fail to please the fancy, and gain approbation.

Having no correct edition of any poem in the language, we can only in general observe what measures their poets employ, and recommend regularity and method to future writers. Since vocal effort by nature is the same in all languages, the Galic measures by the same feet as every other tongue; viz. Dactyles, Spondees, Iambs, Trochees, &c.

Dactyle -ᴗᴗ, one long, and two short syllables; as, *aithrachas*, repentance; *dleasdanach*, dutiful; *bachlagach*, of, or belonging to curling locks.

Spondee --, two long syllables; as, *iomlan*, perfect; *oscion*, above.

Iamb ᴗ-, a short and a long syllable; *coineal*, a candle.

Trochee -ᴗ, one long, and one short syllable; as, *samhradh*, summer; *geamhradh*, winter; *carrach*, spring; *faomhar*, harvest; *crabhach*, religious.

Of the different Sorts of Poetry.

Heroics of ten feet are generally iambs; thus,

Neamhidh! mar dhriuchd anuas an iocſhlaint taom,
Us, ann an geal-fhath, fiol an fhras go caoin!
Le tin's le lag ni cuiduchadh an lus,
O dhoinnunn faſgadh, dubhradh fuar o theas;
Gach eucoir ſguiridh, ſiubhlidh ciontan ſean,
Us togidh Ceartas ris ag tein a meigh;
Mach thar an t faol flat ola ſmidh Sioth,
'S ann truſcan geal theid Neochiontas 'nſin ſios.

The meaſure of Oſſian's poetry is very irregular and various. Generally he has couplets of eight, though they do not rhime, and ſeven, and ſometimes nine ſyllables. Theſe feet are moſt commonly trochee and dactyle. The trochee occupies the firſt, dactyle the ſecond and third, and a long ſyllable ends the line. Thus,

Thanic errach le ſioladh nan ſpeur,
Cho d'eirich duill' uaine dhamh fein.
Chunic oigna me ſamhach 's an talla,
Agus bhuail iad clairſach nam fonn.
Bha deoir ag taomadh le gruaidhan Mhalmhin;
Chunic oigh' me 's mo thuiradh go trom.
C'uim' am bheil thu co tuirſach a' m' fhianuis,
Chaomh Ainnir og Luath-ath nan ſruth?

An ro e fgiamhach mar dhearfa na greine?
Am bu cho tlachdor a fhiubhal's a chruth?
'S taitnach t fhonn ann cluas Offian,
Nighain Lu ath-ath nan fruth dian.
Offian's *Malvina's Dream*.

Thefe lines have beauties that the tranflation, notwithftanding its excellence, has not been able to difplay.

The Editors of the Galic Pfalms confined their meafure to eight and fix fyllables; thus,

Sior-bheannuchibh Dehobha mor,
O! aingla treun ann neart,
Tha deanamh iarrtais mar is coir,
Ag eifdachd re a reachd.   Pfal. ciii. 20.

The following ftanza, from a beautiful ode by Macintyre, though originally wrote to a certain tune, however, preferves a regular return of rhime. The lines are alternately nine and feven fyllables; the fecond and fourth rhime; and fometimes the firft and third.

Do chuach-fhalt ban air fas co barrail,
'S a bhar lan chamag us dhual;
T'aghai ghlan, mhalta, narach, bheanal,
Dho dha chaol-mhala gau ghruaim;
Suil ghorm, liontach, mhin-rofg, mheallach,
Gun di cur fal' ann do ghruaidh,

Dead

Dead gheal iobhri, dhionach, dhaingean,
Beul bidh nach canadh ach ftuaim.

Shiubhladh tu fafach airidh gline,
'S an ait ann cinnadh an fpreidh,
'G am bleothan mu chro ; 's bhith'dh choir na h
　　　innis,
Laoigh og ag miradh 's ag leum ;
Cho mheafa do lamh 's tu lamh ri coinnail
No'n feomar foilleir ri grein,
Ag fuaidhal 's ag faimadh bhan us phionar,
Anrram chur grinnis air greus.

The fame poet, though illiterate, exclufive of his tune, feems to have a defign in making the fecond and fourth, and fometimes the firft and third rhime with each other, as in the preceding example. The following ftanza from his Defcription of Coire Cheathaich, has in the firft line ten, and in the fecond nine fyllables.

'S a' mhaddin chiuin-gheal, ann am dhamh dufgadh,
Aig bun na ftuice b'e 'n fugradh leam :
A' chearc le fgiucan ag gabhal tuchain,
'S an caolach cuirtal ag durdal crom.
An dreathan furdal, 's a riobhaid chiuil aige,
Ag cur nan fmuid dheth go luthor binn,
An truid 's am bru-dhearg, le moran unaich,
Re ceilar fundach bu fhiubhlach rann.

There is a poem compofed by the fame author,
the

the variety of which is singular. It is called Beindorain. The stanzas are very long. The first is recitative; of which the first line is iambic, and consists of seven syllables; the second of four syllables, the three last make a dactyle. The second couplet repeats the same feet, and then goes on in the most diversified measures of dactyle, trochee and iamb. One imagines, on reading them, he sees an army of men on a hasty march; sometimes running, sometimes halting at once, then slowly moving, again running, and stopping at once, in strange variety. Macintyre, in this poem, imitated Macdonald, who wrote two pieces, in the same style, set to Piobairachd——

The following is a specimen from Macintyre:

B'i sin a' mhaoslach luainach,
Feadh oganan;
Biolaichan nan bruach
'S aite comhnuidh dhi,
Duilagan nan craobh,
Criomagan a gaoil,
Cho b' e 'm fotrus.
A h aigna ea-trom suairc,
Aobhach alt gan ghruaim,
Cean bu bhraise, ghuanaiche,
Ghoraiche;
A' chre bu cheanalt stuaim,
Chalich i go buan
Ann glean a' bharaich uaine
Bu nosaire.

Second

Second part, slower.

'S i 'n eilaid bheg, bhinnach,
Bu ghunaiche fraonadh,
Le cuinein geur, biorach,
Ag firadh na gaoithe,
Gafganach, fpeirach,
Feadh chreachan na beine,
Le eagal roi theine,
Cho teirin i aonach, &c.

Third part, flow.

Cho b' aithne dhamh co leanadh i
Do fheara na roin Eorpa,
Mur faicadh e dea-ghean urra,
'S tein farafda 'n a co-dhail,
Go fartach bhith 'n a h earalas,
Tein am faigfe dhi m'an corrnich i,
Go faicilach, gle earralach,
Man fairich i 'n a coir e, &c.

These different meafures are called *urlar*, *fiubhal*, and *An crunluath*.

There is a fpecies of poetry peculiar to the Gael called *Iurram* and *Orain luathaidh*. The mufic of the *Iurram* has always that mixture of grandeur and melancholy that never fails to gain its end. They are fung on board of fhips and buirlings by the failors, when they row or work, to deceive the time. The

fubject

subject is generally the life and actions of some chief or relation. The language is such as to express the sentiments and actions described; the music, expression, and the strokes of the oars, coinciding in such exact time, both the sailor and passenger forget their hardships and fatigue, even in the most inclement seasons. The *Oran luathaidh*, with the same view, is sung when they work on shore, and derives its name from *luthadh*, milling or fulling. Till very lately, fulling of cloth by mills was not known in the Highlands, and in some parts is not yet introduced. They fulled their cloth by laying it wet on an extended frame of rods wattled together, around which were placed as many women as could conveniently be employed, who, by an alternate motion of their feet, kept the cloth in perpetual rotation. One of them, in the mean time, sung the verse, and all the rest at once joined in the chorus. And even at this day, when these songs are sung in genteel company, a lady's handkerchief or a gentleman's bonnet supplies the place of the piece of cloth, every one taking hold of a corner. The time of this species of singing is not so quick as that of the *Reel*, nor so slow as the *Iurram*. It is exceedingly lively, however, and justifies what a French gentleman observed of the Scots music: *La musique Eccossoise sur tout pour le divertissement & toucher le coeur.* The following is a specimen of an *Oran-luathaidh:*

I.

'Togamid fonn air luathadh a chlolain,
Gabhamid ceol us orain mhatha.

Chorus.

Horo gu'n togin air shugan fhathasd,
Horo i io man d'theid mi laidhidh ;
Horo gu'n togin air shugan fhathasd.

II.

B'fhearrd' an clo bhith choir nan gruagach,
Dheanadh an luathadh le 'n lamhan.
  Horo, &c.

III.

Nuair thionduichas iad air cleath e
Chluintadh fuaim gach te dhiu labhairt.
  Horo, &c.

IV.

Orain ghrinne, bhinne, mhisle
Aig na riobhinan 'g an gabhal.
  Horo, &c.

Specimens * *of true Orthography.*

SOLILOQUY.

Sweet is the breath of morn, her rising sweet
With charm of earliest birds————
Milton's Par. Lost, B. IV.

MOCH am maddin shamrich, nuair bha'n t athar fionnor, an talamh tais, agus aghai na Cruthachd, go leir, uror, sgiamhach, dh' erich agus chuaidh mi mach. Is gann bha 'n saol bruinach air mosgladh; cho do chrath Sgios dhe a throm-chodal go leir; agus cho ro Stri ach air aomadh a cin ghuanaich. Bha gach ni feathal. Bha gach ni fonnor. Bha gach ni ag aomadh gu tamh Inntin agus ag brosnuchadh smuainta glic. Threig an Uisog amhain a nead ag eirich
air

---

* I thought it proper to give some pieces in prose and verse, both as specimens of the right Orthography, and as illustrations of my Grammatical System. And here I must observe, that the few books hitherto published in the language, however excellent the composition may otherways be, are so inaccurate in respect of orthography, that I can hardly select one paragraph without making amendments. The Rev. Mr. Macfarlane's translation of Baxter's Call to the Unconverted, printed by Foulis of Glasgow, 1750, is the most accurate that has appeared; but he too has his errata; they are few, however, and when we consider that he had no guide to direct his course, we must ever admire his ingenuity.

air an fgeath dh'altuchadh beatha an nua-la. Air a h arduchadh anns an athar, bha i gairm nam fear-oibre mach, agus a luchd-ciuil fein gu fein. Eoin is moiche gluafachd, thuirt mife, chompanaich na maddin! eiram ghna leatfe! Eiram thairigfin oran na maddin, agus dh'aoradh an Ti mhoir fin a bheir air dol amach na maddin & an fheafcair luath-ghair dheanamh. O! Cia tlachdor dol amach anns an uair mhoch fo! Mhealtin feath Naduir & bhlafachd urorachd na maddin!

Caochluchidh na neoil ghorm uigh air uigh. Dathidh ruidha dearg na fpeuran, gus am fas aghi ghorm na maddin, fadheoi, mar gu bithadh i fgedichte go leir le naire. Am bheil mife fos ann mo chodal? Am bruadar fo? Am feud e bith? No am bheil na fpeura, reradh, dearg le gnuif-naire, uirad do dhaoine fhaicin agus an cin trom-chodlach air aodhartan? An coidal daoine ann focair fhuaimhnach? An caith iad na h uara priofal fin ann leife; nuair tha a' ghrian ann aird & ag dol air gnothach a Cruthior? Nuair tha eunli an athair ag laoi-mholadh De agus ag aoradh le co-fheirm. Oh! na bithadh e mar fo! Duifgamid ni is airde ceol na muintir fo, le guth aoraidh reufonta chur ris. Meadichamid iobairta deagh-bholtrach Naduir, le coimeafc molaidh ar bili-ne is foirfaiche, leis an tuis a tha 'g eirich o'n talamh.

Mar nach bheil toradh, is amhli cho'n 'eil Aoibhnas, no Criodhalachd ann, gan a' ghrian. Nuair chraobh-fgaolas Triach caomh fin an la, Coinolachd a Ghloir-mhaddin,

mhaddin, bithidh na uile Chretoira beathal le a lathair, fuilmhor & aidharach le a thiolacaidh. Eirichidh milte do pheiftogan, chum beatha, d'an grianuchadh ann a ghathana. Cliofgidh na h eoin o an codal & doirtidh iad amach an anaman aoibhnach ann co-fheirm Le meilach bheir na treuda buidhachas air-fon na maddin; agus innfidh an t ealach le ard-gheim-nach taincolachd. Tha na glin ag arris a' chiul fin; agus na cnoic ag fregairt do'n fhonn. Tha gach bith ag am bheil guth ag aontuchadh anns an oran fo; tha gach ni ag am bheil beatha gairdach ann a chliu.

Dhirich mi tuloch agus ghabh mi fealadh do'n Du-thich mancuairt. O! an fealadh a chunic mi! Cia farfin, Cia lan agus pailt anns gach ni! am beartas Naduir go leir! Cia beartach agus neo-thraiach an Tigh-ftoir a tha annfo! Air leamfe gu faicam anns na leabhran fin, eidir-mhinuchadh foilleir air an dea-mholadh fin air mathas De: " Tha Suilan gach ni
" feithamh ort, agus bheir thu dhoibh am biadh ann
" am feim Fofglidh thu do lamh go toirbheartach
" agus fafuchidh thu mian gach ni beo.———"

" Thefe are thy glorious works, Parent of good,
" Almighty! thine this univerfal frame,
" Thus wondrous fair! thyfelf how wondrous then!

Milton.

Air an lamh fo faicam an cuan mor, fairfin gan chrioch, air an feol ioma long, le mairfontachd nan Innfa fad amach, na h aird an near & niar, ag ar freafdal

freafdal le nithe priofol na talmhuin, agus obair riomhach, greante, lamh daoine. Faicam an cuan air am plod cabhlach cogaidh nan riogh; gach aon dibh air a h armadh le Accuin-bhais; fgeduichte le ioma breid geal, ard ann cran; daingan gu conruig mar chaiftal no creug; agus mar mhiol-chu fiubhlach dhol anns an toir.

Ann calladh bualidh long bha fad uain, ag aifig, do a chairdan an ti, ris nach ro duil am feafd. Cruinuchidh an faol, mancuairt, aoibhnach ann Gairdachas an coimharfnaich; agus dfhaicin a' chriodh, bha brifte, air a leighas; nuair tha Miann, Muirne agus Gradh a' chriodh fin, air aifig dha. Chunic mi aon uair iad bha gairdach leofan rinn Gairdachas; bha gul leofan a ghul. Chunic mi gairdachas agus gul, aoibhnas agus bron, le cheile, ag lafadh, agus ag muchadh na h aigne; folas agus dolas ann aon uair ag leighas agus ag briftadh a' chriodh chedn. Chunic mi dis a bha dilis do cheile, re ioma blianadh, air tachairt, nach dealich ni 's mo; agus an lanain bha air an fgarachdin, aris fonadh le cheile. Dh'innis iad ioma fgeul, Soirbhas agus Doirbhas, ris an d'eifd a' chuidachd mhaoth, ag glafadh ma mhuinal an Athair, & ag jarridh tearmuin ann a uchd. Annfin thug iad uile buidhachas agus taing, ag fein Cumhachd & Mathas De, mar leanas.

Tha loingas fiubhal ann go tiugh,
'S an Lebhiaton mor,
A' bheift a dhealbhadh, ainhal, leat,
Re mirag ann le treoir.

Na sloigh od uile tha'd O Dhia!
Ag feithamh ort do ghna,
Do chum gu tugadh tu dhoibh biadh,
D'an cumal beo, gach tra.——Psal. civ. 26, 27.

O! b'fhearr gu moladh daoine Dia,
Airson a mhathais chaoin;
'S airson a bhearta iongantach
Rinn e do chlan nan daoin.
Luchd loingais theid air muir 's a bhith 's,
Re gniomh ann uisgan buan;
Dhoibhsan is leir mor oibra De,
Us iongantais 's a' chuan.
Air Iartas duisgar suas a' ghaoth,
Go ard 's go doineinach;
Le 'n togar suas, go attor, borb,
Na tonna garbh ma seach.
Tha 'd uair gu neamh ag erich suas,
Tha 'd, uair, dol doingan sios,
Ionnus gu d' leagh an nam truagh,
Le triobloid chruaidh, 's le sgios.
Dol, chuig' us uaidh', go tuislach fos,
Amhli mar dhuin' air mhisg,
Ionnus gu d' threig, go builach, iad,
Gach gliocas bha 'n am measg.
Ghlaodh iad, annsin, re Dia 'n an tein,
O'n triobloid shaor e iad;
Us chuiradh, leis, an stoirm, gu feath,
'S na tuin 'n an tamh do bha'd.
Annsin ata iad ait, airson
Gu bheil iad samhach, beo;

'S

'S gu d' thug e iad do'n challadh fin,
'S do'n phort, bu mhiannach leo.

Uime fin.

O! b'fhearr gu moladh daoine Dia,
Airfon a mhathas chaoin;
'S arfon a bhearta iongantach,
Rinn e do chlan nan daoin.—Pfal. cvii. 12,—30.

Iob, Caib xvix. 11,——20.

Nuair chualadh a' chluas me, annfin bheannich i me; agus nuair chunic an t fuil me, thog i fianuis leam.

Chion gu do fhaor mi am bochd a ghlaodh, an dilachd, agus an ti, aig nach ro aon d' a chuiduchadh.

Thanic beannachd an ti bha reidh chum bais orm; agus thug mi air criodh na beantraich, luath-ghair dheanamh.

Chuir mi ionracas umam, agus fgeudich e me; agus bha mo bhreathanas mar chrun, agus mar thrufcan.

Bha mi mar fhuilan do'n dall, agus mar chofan do'n bhacach.

Bha mi 'm m'athair do'n bhochd; agus a' chuis, nach b' aithnadh dhamh, ranfuich mi mach.

Agus bhris mi gial an droch-dhuine; agus tharruin mi an edail as fhiaclan.

Annfin

Annsin thuirt mi, gheibh mi bas ann mo neud; agus meaduchidh mi mo laan mar ghainamh.

Leaduichar mo fhreimh lamh ris na h uisgan, agus *laidhidh* an driuchd, feadh na h oich, air mo bheangan* !

The Speech of Galgacus †, *translated from the Latin of* Tacitus, *in his Life of* Agricola.

Gach uair smuaintas mi air abhar a' chogaidh so, agus an egin anns am bheil sin, tha mo chriodh ag innsadh dhamh, gu cuir an la diugh, ma bhithas sibh uile deonach agus aonintinach, crioch air a' chogadh so, agus gu sgaolar cuibhrach Bhrettuin go leir. Oir bha sin uile, ach beg, ann Daorse, agus cho'n 'eil cearna don tir,	*Quotiens causas belli & necessitatem nostram intueor, magnus mihi animus est, hodiernum diem, consensumque vestrum, initium libertatis totius Britanniæ fore. Nam et universi servitutis expertes: & nulla ultrâ*

T

* It were to be wished, that a complete Translation of the Old and New Testaments were printed according to the Orthography of the above specimen.

† Pronounced at the head of an army of Caledonians, when about to engage the Roman army on the Grampian Hills.

no an fhairge fein, tearuinte
dhuin, nuair tha am plod Romanach bagar oirin. Marso
tha cogadh, us airm, bha ono-
rach do ghaisgaich, anois, mar
dhidan cintach do ghealtairan.
Anns na blair, a chuiradh, roi,
ris na Romanaich nach d'thug
buaidh, bha ar dochas agus ar
bunn ann ar lamhan fein: bhri
gu bu sin a b' uaisle ann am
Brettun uile, agus ann comhnuidh anns a' chearna is faide
mach, nach facadh, riamh,
cladach thrailan, no an fuilan
mio-naomhichte le Antiarnas
fhaicin. Dhion ar n uaignas
sinne, a' chuid is faide mach
do'n t saol, agus a' mhuintir
is deiranaiche aig am bheil
Saorse, gus an la diugh. Anois
tha crioch Bhrettuin 'n ar seal-
ladh; agus is minic tha gach
ni coigrach, agus dorch, mor
agus ainmol. Ach anois cho'n
'eil cinnadh fa-bith air ar cul,
cho 'n 'eil ni ach an fhairge
us na creugan; agus na Romanaich, air ar n aghai, noch
tha sibh, ann diomhanas, ag
feachnadh. Tha iadsan, Spui-

*trà terræ, ac ne maer
quidem securum, im-
minente nobis classe
Romaná, ita prælium
atque arma, quæ for-
tibus honesta, eadem
etiam ignavis tutissi-
ma sunt. Priores
pugnæ, quibus adver-
sus Romanos variâ
fortunâ certatum est,
spem ac subsidium in
nostris manibus ha-
bebant: quia nobilis-
simi totius Britan-
niæ, eoque in ipsis
penetralibus siti, nec
servientium littora as-
picientes, oculos, quo-
que â contactu domi-
nationis inviolatos
habebamus. Nos ter-
rarum ac libertatis
extremos, recessus ip-
se ac sinus famæ in
hunc diem defendit.
Nunc terminus Bri-
tanniæ patet. Atque
omne ignotum, pro
magnifico est. Sed
nulla jam ultrâ gens,
nihil*

THE GALIC LANGUAGE.

nadairan an t saoil go leir, an deigh na tir do fgrios, ag foirfadh na fairge cuidachd. Ma tha an namhid beartach, tha iadfan fantach; ma tha iad bochd, gloirmhiannach; noch nach do fhafuich an aird an Near no an Niar. Do na h uile dhaoine, fantuchidh iadfan, ionnan, beartas agus bochdin. Mortuidh iad, togidh iad creach, agus go eucorach gabhidh iad coir; agus, an deigh duthich fgrios lom, mar fhafach, their iad Sioth-chaint ris. Is e mian Naduir an clan & an cairdan bhith dilis do gach neach: tha iadfan air an toirt uain, gu tir eile, am bruid; agus tha ar mnaan agus ar peithran, ma fheachan iad am mianna naimhdal, ann cairdas & aidh alachd, air am milladh. Thug iad, uaine, ar n arnais agus ar cuid, mar dheachbhidh, agus ar graine mar inlidh. Caithidh iad ar cuirp & ar lamhan gearradh choiltan & glanadh mhointach, fo mhafladh & fo bhuillan. Tha daoine faor, rugadh chum trailalachd,

nihil nisi fluctus & faxa; & interiores Romani. Quorum superbiam frustra per obsequium & modestiam effugeris. Raptores orbis, postquam cuncta vastantibus defuere terræ, & mare scrutantur: si locuples hostis est, avari: si pauper, ambitiosi. Quos non Oriens, non Occidens, satiaverit: soli omnium, opes atque inopiam pari effectu concupiscunt. Auferre, trucidare, rapere falsis nominibus imperium: atque ubi solitudinem faciunt, pacem appellant. Liberos cuique ac propinquos suos natura cariffimos esse voluit: hi per dilectus alibi servituti auferuntur. Conjuges, fororesque, & si hostilem libidinem effugiant, nomi-

ne

air an ceannach, aon uair, a-gus air am beathuchadh le am maistiran; ach tha Brettun, gach la, ceannachd a daorfe fein, gach la ag a beathuchadh. Agus ann an Tealach mar tha gach aon is deiranaiche thig, mar chulidh-fanoid do'n mhuintir eile; ceart mar fin anns an tealach fo is fine air thalamh, tha finne, is deiranaiche agus is truailidhe, air bord ar fgrios. Agus cho 'n 'eil aginne fearan no mitailte, no calladh chum an d'theid fin. Tuile fos, tha mifnach treunas & runachd nan iocran neothaitnach do na h uachdrain; mar is moa tha fibhfe tearuinte, is moa an amharasfan. Uime fin, o tha ar dochas air a chall, fadheoi glacibh-fe mifuach leis an cominach flainte & faorfe ri onoir & urram. Fo cheanfalachd mna, chuir na Brigantaich teine ri an aituchas, agus ghlac iad an daingnuchais. Agus mur bhithadh gu do thiondaidh iad an dea-fhortun gu leifg, thilgadh iad dhibh an

ne amicorum atque hofpitum poluuntur. Bona fortunafque in tributum egerunt; in annonam, frumentum. Corpora ipfa ac manus, fylvis ac paludibus emuniendis, verbera inter ac contumelias, conterunt. Nata fervituti mancipia femel veneunt, atque ultro â dominis aluntur: Britannia fervitutem fuam quotidie emit, quotidie pafcit. At ficut in familiâ recentiffimus quifque fervorum & confervis ludibrio eft: fic in hoc orbis terrarum vetere famulatu, novi nos & viles in excidium petimur. Neque enim aura nobis, aut metalla, aut portus funt, quibus exercendis refervemur. Virtus porro ac ferocia fubjectorum, ingrata imperantibus

THE GALIC LANGUAGE.

cuibhrach. Ach sinne slan agus neo-chuibhrichte, cho 'n 'eil sin ag stribh airson ar saorse fein, ach leigidh sin fhaicin do'n t saol, anns a' chiad dol siois ciod iad na fir a chuir Albin amach. An creid sibh gu bheil misnach, ann cogadh, aig na Romanaich, mar tha iad uailol le bosd & antiarnas ann siothchaint! Ma sgaras sinne & ma bhithas sin, le mi-chordadh, iom-reusonach, bithidh iadsan mor; oir is e gealtairachd an namhaid gloir an armailte-san; mar saol sibh gu coimheadtadh na Francaich & na Germanaich, agus (narach innsadh!) a' chuid is moa do na Brettunaich toirt fola do choigraich, ni is faide mar naimhdan no mar thrailan, air an onoir agus an gradh. Is lag am bann gaoil eagal & oilt; noch nuair bhuinas tu as, gabhidh iadsan fuath, ag sgur bhith eagalach roimhad. Tha gach ni ag

& longinquitas ac secretum ipsum quo tutius, eo suspectius. Ita sublatâ spe veniæ, tandem sumite animum, tam quibus salus, quàm quibus gloria carissima est. Brigantes, femina duce, exurere coloniam, expugnare castra: ac nisi felicitas in secordiam vertisset, exuere jugum potuere: nos integri & indomiti & libertatem non in præsentia laturi, primo statim congressu unde ostendamus quos sibi Caledonia viros seposuerit. An eandem Romanis in bello virtutem, quam in pace lasciviam adesse creditis? Nostris illi dissensionibus ac discordiis clari, vitia hostium in gloriam exercitus sui vertunt: quem contractum ex diversissimis gentibus, ut secundæ res tenent, ita adversæ dissolvent. Nisi si Gallos, & Germanos, & (pudet dictu)

ar brofnuchadh, agus ag gealtuin buaidh dhuin; ach fin fein bhith deonach: cho 'n 'eil am mnaan ag brofnuchadh nan Romanach: cho 'n 'eil cairdan miomholadh an teithaidh. Ma tha tir acca is coimhach i: Tha na Dea toirt dhuinne, go conruic, began, eglach le aineolas, ag fealtin neaimh agus thallaimh, nan coiltan, na fairge agus ga ch ni nach aithnuich iad. Na cuiradh nithe faoin egal oiribh: lannir an oir, agus follus an airgaid, nach dion, agus nach loit! Gheibh fin ar treife ann airmailta nan naimhdan. Seafadh na Brettunaich an cuis fein! Cuimhnuchidh na Francaich an faorfe o chian. Treigidh a' chuid eiled o na Germanaich iad mar rinn na Ufipianaich cheanadh. Anois cho 'n 'eil ni chur egail oiribh, ach daingnaich gan daoine; tirachaidh do fhean-daoine, meafg iocrain cheanair-cach & uachdrain

tu) Britannorum plerofque dominationi alienæ fanguinem commodantes, diutius tamen hoftes quam fervos, fide & affectu teneri putatis: metus & terror eft, infirma vincula caritatis; quæ ubi removeris, qui timere defierint, odiffe incipient. Omnia victoriæ incitamenta pro nobis funt: nullæ Romanos conjuges accendunt: nulli parentes fugam exprobraturi funt: aut nulla plerifque patria, aut alia eft: paucos numero circum trepidos ignorantia, cælum ipfum ac mare & filvas ignota omnia circumfpectantes, claufos quodammodo ac vinctos alii nobis tradiderunt. Ne terreat vanus afpectus: & auri fulgor atque argenti, quod neque tegit, neque vulnerat. In ipfa hoftium acie inveniemus noftras manus. Agnofcent Britanni

neo-laghal. Is iad sin ar n aii mailta, is mise bhar ceanart ; annsin tha bhar deach bhidh, bhar cuibhrach, agus gach pianas thrailan, a dfheudas sibh air a' mhachaire so mhealtuin re bhar beo; no thilgin dhibh go siorruidh. Nois, fadheoi, chuimnuchibh air mead bhar fola agus daoine, bhar saorse fein agus bhar tir; cuimhnuchibh bhar sinsira, sibh fein, bhar sliochd, agus leanibh mise.

ni suam causam. Recordabuntur Galli priorem libertatem. Deserent illos ceteri Germani, tamquam nuper Usipii reliquerunt. Nec quidquam ultra formidinis, vacua castella, senum coloniæ, inter male parentes & injuste imperantes, ægra municipia & metalla, & ceteræ servientium pœnæ: quas in æternum proferre, aut statim ulcisci, in hoc campo est. Proinde ituri in aciem & majores vestros, & posteros cogitate.

MOTHUCHADH.

O mhothuchaidh ghraidh! thobair neo-thraiaich gach ni tha luachor 'n ar subhachas, no costal 'n ar dubhachas! ceanglidh thu sios air leabe chonlaich e fhear-fianuis, agus is tuse dhuisgas e suas gu neamh. O! thobair shiorruidh ar fulaing! Is annso lorgaras mi thu, agus is i so do bhith neamhidh, tha gluasachd ann taobh stigh dhiom: " Ge do chriopas m'anam, " ann ioma uair thuirsach, thin, air ais; agus chlis- " gas e air iomradh bhasorachd!"—focuil mhor!— Ach, gach subhachas agus curam mor, agus uasal, a
mhothuchas

mhothuchas mi, is uaitse thig iad uile, O mhorchriodh an domhain! a ghluaisas ma thuitas roine d'ar cean anns a' chearne is faide mach do d' chruithachd. Air a bhrofnuchadh leatse, tairnidh Eugenius mo chuirtinan, nuair tha mi fann; eisdidh e ri m' ghearan, agus coiruchidh e an aimsir airson a thinais. Bheir thu cuibhran dhe, cor uair, do'n bhuachil is suaraiche 's na mulaich. Tachridh e ris an uan, do threud fir-eile, a loitadh. Anns a' mhinnaid so, chunic mi e leagin a chin air a lorg-bhuachail, agus, le aomadh tuirsach, ag amharc air. O an tigin ach minnaid ni bu luaithe! tha e call fuil a chriod—tha fuil a chriodhsan sioladh leis.

Siothchaint dhuit, bhuachail uasail! chibh mi thu ag imachd ann dubhachas. Ach ao tromuchidh do shubachas aon la thu! Oir is sona do bhochan, agus is sona do chompanach, agus is sona na h uain ni mire mancuairt duit.

SENSIBILITY.

Dear Sensibility! source inexhausted of all that is precious in our joys, or costly in our sorrows! thou chainest thy martyr down upon his bed of straw, and it is thou who liftest him up to heaven. Eternal fountain of our feelings! It is here I trace thee, and this is thy divinity that stirs within me: not that in some sad and sickening moments "my soul shrinks "back upon herself, and startles at destruction;" mere

pomp

pomp of words! but that I feel some generous joys and generous cares beyond myself; all come from thee, great, great sensorium of the world, which vibrates, if a hair of our head falls to the ground, in the remotest desart of thy creation. Touched with thee, Eugenius draws my curtain when I languish; hears my tale of symptoms, and blames the weather for the disorders of his nerves. Thou givest a portion of it sometimes to the roughest peasant, who traverses the bleakest mountains. He finds the lacerated lamb of another's flock. This moment I behold him leaning with his head against his crook, with piteous inclination looking down upon it. Oh! had I come one moment sooner! it bleeds to death; his gentle heart bleeds with it.

Peace to thee, generous swain! I see thou walkest off with anguish; but thy joys shall balance it; for happy is thy cottage, and happy is the sharer of it, and happy are the lambs which sport about you.—
STERNE.

Mr Pope's MESSIAH *translated into Galic Rhime.*

Inghina Shalem! duifgibh nois an ceol;
Dh'orana neamhidh 'n guth is aird' is coir,
Aftina Phinduis us nam maidanan,
Dubhradh nan craobh, us fuarana nam beann,
Ni 's mo cho 'n ail —Mo ghuth, anois duifg thus'
Ri bili naomh Ifaias bhuin air thus.

Gu uairan eile faicin ghlaodh am bard:
Torchidh maidan, 's beiridh maidan mac!
Feuch! eir'chidh beangan, mach o fhreimhach Iefs,
Feadh fpeuran, chuiras dea-bholadh, le bhlaths'.
Us air a dhuille trialidh 'n fpiorad naomh,
Air bhar ni tuirlin 'n colum diamhir, caomh.
Neamha! mar dhriuchd, anuas, an ioc-fhlaint, taom,
Us, ann an geal-fhath, fiol an fhras go caoin!
Le tin, 's le lag ni cuiduchadh an lus,
O dhoinunn fafgadh, dubhradh fuar, o theas.
Gach eucoir fguiridh, fiubhlidh ciontan fean,
Us togidh Ceartas, ris ag tein, a meigh;
Mach, thar an t faol, flat-ola finidh Sioth,
'S ann trufcan geal theid Neochiontas 'nfin fios.
Seachad na blianaidh, eiradh mhaddin ait!
O! leim gu follus, leanaibh chaoimh bith breit.
Tha Nadur, luath, ag deifruchadh a gibht,
Curthachd fos, 's, do ghna, a tuis, ag fibht:
Faic togal fuas a chean ard Lebanon,
Faic air na cnoic ag damhfadh cranna trom:
Faic neoil, lan fpios, ag eirigh fuas o Sharon,
Is luf-mhaoth Carmel dea-bholadh nan fpeuran!
Eifd! air an fhafach thiamhidh, tha guth ait;
Gleufibh an t fligh' tha Dia, tha Dia ag teachd:
Dia! Dia ag teachd 'nfin fhreagair guth nan creug,
Us ghlaodh na beantan, labhairt, Dia ag teachd.
Bith'bh iofal fhleibhta, eiradh ard na glin,
Tha 'n faol 'g a ghabhal, o na neamhdha, tein!
Umhlachd, bhar bar crom, Shedair thugibh dho,
Coinhrad chairga, uifgan bras dean rod!

Cluinidh

Cluinidh am balbh, tha 'n flanioir ag teachd,
Gheal baird o fhean! an dall chibh e gle air.
O fgiathan tiugh an t amharc glanidh e,
Air chlach-fhuil dhorch an la togidh e:
Bheir do na cluafa duinte guth gu cluin;
Us oran nuadh air fonna, ceolor, binn,
Seinidh am balbh; gan trofnan criplach theid
Uallach, thar altan leim, mar mhac an fheidh.
Gearan no cumhadh, 's an t faol, cho bhith, ni 's mo,
O'n fuilan uile glanidh e na deoir.
Ann geamhlan cruaidh, 'nfin, ceanlar fios am bas,
'S ann Antiara gruamach iofrain gath theid fas.
Mar threudich math a choimhdas cruin na caoraidh,
Innaltradh nuadh bhith's, go tric, ag iarridh,
Chaoidhas luchd cailt, luchd feachrain threoruichas,
'S an oiche ghleadhas, 's an la innaltras ;
Na uain og togidh fuas, 'n a lamh, go caomh,
Gach aon ag altram, ann a uchd mar naomh;
Marfo mor-churam, do an chinadh-dhaon,
Gabhidh Ath'r caomh nan lin a tha 'n ar deidh.
Ni 's mo, cho 'n eirich riochd, ann aghai riochd,
Ni 'n tachir gaifgaich, tograch, le aniochd;
Air magha, fos, cho'n fhaicar iana glas,
Cho duifg, ni 's mo, fuaim ftuic ard-fhearg, gu cath.
Na lain, gan fheim, 'n an corrain nitar crom,
Do'n chlaidhamh da-laimh nitar coltair trom.
'Nfin palluina theid fuas, us ni am mac,
Lan aoibhnach, 'ni fin thofich ath'r o fhean ;
An craobha fion, d'an fliochd fein, dubhradh bheir,
'S, an lamh a thug go toirbheartach, 'nfin gheibh.
Ionadh an treudich glacidh 'm fafach lom,
Nuair chibh e feur, us neonain, fas fo bhonn;
Cliofgidh,

Cliofgidh, nuair, meafg nan carruig, thartor, chruaidh,
Ni eafan, leimnach, monar ann a chluais.
Ann garraidh chruaidh, roi garradh dion nan dragon,
Air chrith tha cuilc, us luachir turadan.
Meafg ghlean thartor, cuirinichte le dreas,
Tha giubhas birach, us cran buicfe deas;
'N ait lom-phreas fafidh, dofrach, an cran dait,
'S am miortal boltrach far ro droch-luinach.
Air magha gorm le mic-tir theid na h uain,
'S an tiogar fdiuridh clan bheg meafg nan cluan;
Gluaifidh le cheil, an leoghan us an damh,
Us glanidh nathair cos nan taifgalach;
An leanabh, beadradh, togidh ann a lamh
Na dearca ballach, us an Nathair neimh,
Toilichte, fealidh lannir uain an fcoil,
'S le 'n teangadh chrocach, agus gath, ni fpors.
Eirich o Shalem! tha le follus crunt',
Do chean ard tog! na bith'dh do fhuila duint'.
Faic mic. us nighana, tha 'ndiugh gan bhreith,
Faic feadh, do chùirt, na h ail a tha gan bhith,
Am buidh'nan cruin, ag eirich, air gach taobh,
Ag iarridh beatha, deonach bhith air neamh.
Faic ducha coimhach, gu do dhoirfa, teithadh,
Trial ann do fhollus, ann do theampul feithadh;
Ma t' altair ghraonach tha na riogha cruin,
Us gibhta trom do fhas nan Sabean!
'S ann dhuits' air fpiofa Idume, tha blath,
Us mein an oir am beanta Ophir fas.
Faic doirfa neaimh, go graonach, fofgladh dhut;
Us meadhon-la go foilfach, 'g eirich ort.
Ni 's mo cho dath a' ghrian a' mhaddin chiuin,

No

No mhaddinog, no teachd an 't foluis uir;
Ach dorch, us foluicht' ann an dealradh glan
Solluis do chuirt-fe, tha gach follus fann;
'S leat fein an la! foilfach, ur, do ghna!
Lochran o neamh, bheir follus dhuit go brach.
Trath'chidh an cuan, mar dheatach trialidh neoil,
Mar dhus gach creug, leaghidh na cnoic mar cheir,
Ach fhocal daingan us a chumhachd treun,
Mairidh do riochd, riaghlidh Meffiah fein!

MALVINA's DREAM, by OSSIAN.

'S e guth anaim mo ruin a tha 'nn,
O! 's ainmach gu aiflin Mhalmhin' thu,
Fofgluibh-fe talla nan fpeur,
Aithra Ofcair nan cruaidh-bheum;
Fofgluibh-fe doirfa nan nial,
Tha ceumma Mhalmhine go dian.
Chualam guth a' m' aiflin fein,
Tha fathrum mo chleibh go ard.
C' uime thanic an Offag a' m' dheigh
O dhubh-fhiubhal na linne od thall?
   Bha do fgiath fhuimnach ann gallan an aonaich,
Shiubhall aiflin Mhalhine go dian,
Ach chunic is' a run ag aomadh,
'S a cheo-earradh ag aomadh m' a chliabh:
Bha dearfa na greine air thaobh ris,
Co boifgal ri or nan daimh.

'S e guth anaim mo ruin a tha 'nn,
O! 's ainmach gu m' aiſlin fein thu.
'S comhnuidh dhuit anam Mhalmhine,
Mhic Oſſain is treine lamh.
Dh'eirich m' ofna marri dearſa o near,
Thaom mo dheoir meaſg ſhioladh na h oiche.
Bu ghallan Aluin a' t fhianuis mi Oſcair,
Le m' uile gheuga uaine ma m' thimchiol?
Ach thanic do bhas-ſa mar Oſſaig
O 'n fhaſach, us dhaom mi ſios.

 Thanic earrach le ſioladh nan ſpeur,
Cho d'eirich duill' uaine dhamh fein;
Chunic oigha me ſamhach 's an talla,
Agus bhuail iad clairſach nan fonn.
Bha deoir ag taomadh le gruaidhan Mhalmhine;
Chunic oigh me 's mo thuiradh gu trom.
C' uime am bheil thu co tuirſach, a' m' fhianuis,
Chaomh Ainnir-og Luath-ath nan ſruth.
An ro e ſgiamhach mar dhearſa na greine?
Am bu cho tlachdor a' ſhiubhal 's a chruth?
'S taitnach t fhonn an cluais Oſſain,
Nighain Luath-ath nan ſruth dian.

 Thanic guth nam bard nach beo,
Am meaſg t aiſlin air aomadh nan ſliabh,
Nuair thuit codal air do ſhuilan ſoirbh,
Aig cuan mor-ſhruth nan ioma fuaim,
Nuair phil thu flathal o 'n t ſeilg,
'S grian la thu ag ſgaolta na bein.——
Chual thu guth nam bard nach beo:
'S glan faital do chiuil fein.
'S caoin faital nam fonn o Mhalmhine!

Ach

THE GALIC LANGUAGE.

Ach claonidh iad anam gu deoir;
Tha folas ann Tuiradh le fioth,
Nuair dh'aomas cliabh tuirfe gu bron;
Ach claoidhih fad-thuirfe fiol dorthuin,
Fhlath nighain Ofcair nan cruaidh-bheum.
'S ainmach an la gan nial
Thuitas iad, mar chuifag, fo 'n ghrian,
Nuair fheallas i fios 'n a foilfe,
Andeigh do'n dubh cheathach fiubhal do'n bheinn,
'S a throm-chean fo fhioladh na h oiche.

TRANSLATION.

IT was the voice of my love! few are his vifits to the Dreams of Malvina! Open your airy halls, ye fathers of mighty Tofcar! unfold the gates of your clouds. The fleps of Malvina's departure are nigh. I have heard a voice in my dream. I feel the fluttering of my foul. Why didft thou come, O blaft, from the dark rolling of the lake? Thy ruftling was in the trees, the dream of Malvina departed. But fhe beheld her love, when his robe of mift flew on the wind; the beam of the fun was on his fkirts, they glittered like the gold of the ftranger. It was the voice of my love; few are his vifits to Malvina.

But thou dwelleft in the foul of Malvina, fon of mighty Offian. My fighs arife with the beams of the eaft; my tears defcend with the drops of night. I was a lovely tree in thy prefence, Ofcar, with all my

branches

branches round me; but thy death came like a blast from the desart, and laid my green head low; the Spring returned with its showers, but no leaf of mine arose. The virgins saw me silent in the hall, and they touched the harp of joy. The tear was on the cheek of Malvina: the virgins beheld me in my grief. Why art thou sad, thou first of the maids of Lutha? was he lovely as the beam of the morning, and stately in thy sight?

Pleasant is thy song in Ossian's ear, daughter of streamy Lutha! Thou hast heard the music of departed bards in the dream of thy rest, when sleep fell on thine eyes, at the murmur of Moruth. When thou didst return from the chace, in the day of the sun, thou hast heard the music of the bards, and thy song is lovely. It is lovely, O Malvina, but it melts the soul. There is a joy in grief, when peace dwells in the breast of the sad. But sorrow wastes the mournful, O daughter of Toscar, and their days are few. They fall away like the flower on which the sun looks in his strength, after the mildew has passed over, and its head is heavy with the drops of night.

Claidhamh

Claidhamh Guth-ullin, *or the Sword of* Guchullin.

Chuir e an claidhamh, fada, fiorchruaidh,
Fulanach, tean, tainic, geur,
'S a chean air a chur ann go focair,
Mar chuis mholta gan dochair lein,
'S e go dirach, diafadach, dubh-ghorm,
'S e cultuidh, cumtadh, conalach,
Go leathan, liobhadh, liobharadh,
Go focair, fafdadh, fo-bhuailte,
Air laimh-chli a' ghaifgaich;
Gur aifaiche do naimhdan a fheachnadh,
No tachairt ris 's an am fin;
Cho bu lughe no cnoc fleibh,
Gach ceum a dheanadh an gaifgach.

TRANSLATION *by Sir* James Foulis, *Bart.*

He feiz'd his fword, thick, broad, and long,
Well forg'd, well hammer'd, temper'd ftrong,
Polifh'd, of pureft metal made,
Like lightning blaz'd the fhining blade;
Jagg'd like a faw, it tore and hewed,
Inur'd to flaughter, blood embrued;
Dire horror, and deftructive fate,
On the fell edge attentive wait;
'Twas certain death its ftroke to feel;
Strength-withering, life-devouring fteel,

Ev'n valiant foes, struck at the sight,
Durst hope no safety but by flight;
Their ranks wide scattering all abroad,
From hill to hill the hero strode.

ODE *from a MS. Collection in the Possession of Miss* Campbell *of* Blandfield.

'S luaimnach mo chodal an nochd,
Ge beo mi, cho bheo mo thlachd,
Mo chriodh air fearg ann 'm uchd,
'S trom dubhach m' intin go beachd.
'S anns an arach, annso shios,
'Tha bean is meachire, min-gheal cruth,
Deud air dhreach cailc 'n a beul,
Bu bhinne no teud-chiuil a guth.
Mar chobhar an uifge ghloin,
Mar fhlios eala ri uifge mear,
Glan leug mar an cathamh-cuir
D'fhag thu me gan chobhair ann d' dheigh.
Slat ur nam faina fionn,
Bean is mine, moghar, fuil,
'S a gruaidh, mar an caoran dearg,
Air lafadh mar dhealbh an rois.
Meoir fhionn air bhafa ban,
Uchd follus is aile fnuadh,
An gaol a thug mi dhi r'a luadh
Ochon nan och, is cruaidh an cas!

Cho

Cho dirich mi aonach no bein,
Mo cheum air a lagadh go trom,
Aighar cho tig air mo ghnuis,
Gus an dean an uir me flan.
Mar ghraine mulaich na deis,
Mar ghallan 's an og-choille fas,
Mar ghrian ri folach nan reul,
Bu thu fein am measg nam mna.

A VOCABULARY of PRIMITIVES.

[m. represents masculine, f. feminine, 1. first declension, and 2. the second. The genitive of each noun is given at full length for the satisfaction of those who chuse to study the language, and to exemplify the rules and method to the Galic Reader.]

Substantive Nouns.

Abhar, abhair, m. 1.	a cause.
Accair, m. 2.	an anchor.
Adharc, adhairc, f. 2.	a horn.
Amadan, amadain, m. 1.	a fool.
Alt, uilt, m. 1.	a joint, sinew.
Aosdan, aosdain, m. 1.	a seer.
Aodan, aodain, m. 1.	the face.
Aran, arain, m. 1.	bread.
Aros, arois, m. 1.	an habitation.
Arm, airm, m. 1.	arms, army.
Arnais, arnais, f. 2.	stores.
Bard, baird, m. 2.	a poet.
Ball, buill, m. 1.	a ball, a place.
Bannis, bainnse, f. 2.	a wedding.
Bith, bith, f. 2.	being.
Bo, bo, f. 2. (pl. *ba.*)	a cow.
Boc, buic, m. 1.	a buck.
Bonn, buinn, m. 1.	a base, sole.

Bord,

Bord, buird, m. 1.	a board, table.
Cabag, cabaig, f. 2.	a cheese.
Cabar, cabair, m. 1.	a pole.
Caoradh, caoraidh, f. 1.	a sheep.
Cean, cin, m. 1.	the head.
Ceist, ceist, f. 2.	a question.
Cos, cois, f. 2.	a foot.
Damh, daimh, m. 1.	a bullock.
Dealg, dilg, m. 1.	a wire, pin.
Dorus, doruis, m. 2.	a door.
Eagal, eagail, m. 1.	fear.
Edal, edail, f. 2.	a treasure.
Eolas, eolais, m. 1.	knowledge.
Fabhar, fabhair, m. 1.	a favour.
Focul, focuil, m. 1.	a word.
Falluin, falluin, f. 2.	a cloak.
Feusag, feusaig, f. 2.	a beard.
Gaoth, gaoith, f. 2.	the wind.
Geilt, geilt, f. 2.	terror.
Gille, gille, m. 2.	a voice.
Glean, glin, m. 1.	a valley.
Ial, eil, f. 2.	a strap, a thong.
Iasg, eisg, m. 2.	a fish.
Iarrun, iarrruin, m. 1.	iron.
Itag, itaig, f. 2.	a feather.
La, la, (pl. laan), m. 2.	a day.
Lamh, laimh, m. 2.	the hand.
Lann, lainn, m. 1.	a sword.
Laoch, laoich, m. 1.	an hero.
Leac, lic, m. 2.	a slate, a stone.
Mac, mic, m. 1.	a son.

Madadh,

Madadh, madaidh, m. 1.   a dog.
Meire, meire, m. 2.   a troop.
Meall, mill, m. 1.   an heap.
Mias, meis, m. 2.   a platter, dish.
Muc, muic, m. 2.   a sow.
Nadur, Naduir, m. 1.   nature.
Neas, nis, m. 2.   a weasel.
Olc, uile, m. 1.   evil.
Osnadh, osnaidh, f. 1.   a sigh.
Or, oir, m.   gold.
Oire, oire, m. 2.   an heir.
Paluin, paluin, f. 2.   a temple.
Paisde, paisde, m. 2.   a child.
Pian, pein, f. 2.   pain.
Piobair, piobair, m. 2.   a piper.
Rann, rainn, m. 2.   a verse.
Ridir, ridir, m. 2.   a knight.
Rinnag, rinnaig, f. 2.   a star.
Riogh, riogh, m. 2.   a king.
Sac, saic, m. 1.   a bag, a sack.
Sogairt, sagairt, m. 2.   a priest.
Sliabh, sleibh, m. 2.   a mountain.
Searag, searaig, f. 2.   a battle.
Talla, talla, f. 2.   a hall.
Tanas, tanais, m. 1.   a ghost.
Tigh, tigh, m. 2.   a house.
Tir, tir, f. 2.   a country.
Ton, tuinn, f. 2.   a wave.
Ubhal, ubhail, f. 2.   an apple.
Uchd, uchd, m. 2.   the breast.
Udar, udair, m. 2.   an author.

Urnuidh, urnuidh, f. 2.   a prayer.
Urlar, urlair, m.   a floor.

Adjective Nouns.

Aghor,	lucky, fortunate.
Alloil,	renowned.
Alluin,	handsome.
Amidach,	foolish.
Balbh,	dumb.
Beanol,	like a woman, modest.
Basor,	mortal.
Beg,	little.
Cam,	crooked.
Caintach,	talkative.
Coir,	just, honest.
Caomh,	dear, beloved.
Dall,	blind.
Dan,	bold, forward, impudent.
Daingan,	tight, strong.
Deas,	neat.
Doirbh,	cross, difficult.
Eaglach,	timorous.
Eolach,	intelligent.
Imchuidh,	fit, proper.
Iongantach,	wonderful.
Iochdor,	merciful.
Gradhach,	loving.
Geur,	edged, sharp, sour.
Goirt,	sore, sour.

Gleuse,

Gleufde,	tuneful, agreeable.
Garbh,	rough, robuſt.
Furafde,	eaſy.
Farfin,	wide.
Fuilach,	bloody.
Follaifach,	public.
Lag,	weak.
Laidir,	ſtrong.
Lionor,	numerous.
Leonte,	wounded.
Luthor,	of much ſtrength.
Math,	good.
Mall,	ſlow.
Mifgach,	drunken.
Muladach,	ſorrowful.
Naomh,	holy.
Neo-ghlan,	unclean.
Narach,	ſhameful.
Obbuin,	ſudden.
Ocrach,	hungry.
Og,	young.
Pailt,	plentiful.
Peccach,	ſinful.
Priofol,	precious.
Ramhar,	fat.
Reubach,	that tears.
Riach,	grey.
Reidh,	eaſy, ready.
Samhach,	quiet.
Santach,	covetous.
Sgiamhach,	beautiful.

Sona,	happy, blessed.
Tana,	thin.
Tarbhach,	substantial.
Tuirsach,	sad.
Treun,	valiant.
Uaibhrach,	high-minded.
Uailol,	boasting.
Uramach,	honourable.

Verbs.

It has been already observed, that the Dative Case of the present participle, or that gerundive which signifies action, is the present of the infinitive. *Dh* therefore begins verbs beginning with a vowel, and *h* is put after the initial consonants in those that begin with consonants.

Dh'abachadh,	to ripen.
Dh'aitachadh,	to inhabit.
Bhathadh,	to drown.
Bheannuchadh,	to bless.
Chabbadh,	to indent.
Chaidradh,	to embrace.
Chomhairlachadh,	to advise.
Dhamhsadh,	to dance.
Dhearmad,	to forget.
Dhealradh,	to shine.
Dh'eisdachd,	to hear.
Dfhuadachadh,	to elope with.
Dfhairadh,	to watch.
Ghabhal,	to take, receive.

Ghearradh,

Ghearradh,	to cut.
Ghlafadh,	to lock, feal.
Dh'iarruidh,	to afk, feek.
Dh'imthachd,	to depart.
Dh'iomain,	to drive.
Labhairt,	to fpeak.
Lamfachadh,	to handle.
Lafadh,	to light, kindle.
Mholadh,	to praife.
Mheaduchadh,	to multiply.
Neartachadh,	to ftrengthen.
Naomhachadh,	to fanctify.
Phaighadh,	to pay.
Pheccachadh,	to fin.
Ranfuchadh,	to fearch.
Reic,	to fell.
Shantachadh,	to covet.
Sheafadh,	to ftand.
Sdiuradh,	to direct, to fteer.
Sgrobadh,	to fcratch.
Shlugadh,	to fwallow.
Smachdachadh,	to correct.
Thagradh,	to defend a caufe.
Theagafg,	to teach.
Thogal,	to lift.
Thoirt,	to give.
Dh'uifgachadh,	to water.
Dh'urachadh,	to refresh, renew.

F I N I S.

www.ingramcontent.com/pod-product-compliance
Lightning Source LLC
Chambersburg PA
CBHW022115160426
43197CB00009B/1027